AF326587

PERMISSION TO BE DIFFERENT

THE AUTISTIC JOYOLOGIST

PERMISSION TO BE DIFFERENT

Create a Happy, Successful Life
Without the Struggle

THE AUTISTIC JOYOLOGIST

Nikki Butler

authors
AND CO.

First published in Great Britain in 2024
by Authors & Co.
www.authorsandco.pub

Copyright © Nikki Butler 2024

Nikki Butler asserts the moral right to be identified as the author of this work in accordance with the Copyright, Designs and Patents Act 1988.

ISBN 978-1-915771-80-3 (paperback)
ISBN 978-1-915771-81-0 (hardback)

To my faithful coffee machine – for the countless early mornings.

To the playlists that got me through the highs and lows.

And to my cat Maverick, who firmly believes that walking across the keyboard is the best way to contribute to my writing. I couldn't have done it without you.

CONTENTS

INTRODUCTION

Have you always felt a bit... different? That you don't quite fit in?

You go to great lengths to cover up the parts of yourself you don't want others to see. You fear being judged, rejected, or perceived as not good enough, so you constantly over–deliver and put others' needs before your own. Despite constant efforts to fit in and be accepted, you feel more isolated and alone than ever. You wonder what's wrong with you and try harder to behave like everyone else.

Does this sound familiar? You're not alone.

It could be that you are neurodivergent. Maybe you are 'just' a bit quirky. The labels are not the important thing.

When you truly understand and accept yourself, and give yourself permission to be different, you can use your unique skills and talents to create a life where you thrive and feel happy. You can stop living life on other people's terms. This freedom will transform both your personal and work life. You will have the confidence to show up with authenticity and without apology.

I was diagnosed as autistic and having ADHD in my mid-forties. In the months that followed my diagnosis, I felt even more isolated and disconnected than ever before. I tried to connect with the true me and open up to others about my diagnosis but many of the people and things that felt familiar to me fell away.

I spent my entire life feeling as though I didn't belong or fit in and that I was fundamentally broken in some way. I struggled with relationships and friendships, endured bullying and exclusion as an adult and failed to find my place in the corporate world, which ended with a traumatic yearlong burnout when I was thirty–six.

I struggled with basic daily tasks that others found easy and concluded that I was 'rubbish at adulting'. My life was a constant battle. Maybe you feel this way too?

At the time of my diagnosis, I ran a multi-award-winning specialist skin and scar clinic. Rather, it ran me. I felt out of control, overwhelmed, unhappy and anxious. All my energy went into my work, and I had no capacity for enjoyment in any other area of my life.

When I couldn't find the answers or help I needed through the tools and techniques everyone told me 'should' work, I panicked. I was terrified. I didn't have the stamina for, potentially, another forty years of these struggles. I had to find my own way forward.

I knew with all my heart that I had to take action to ensure future generations of autistic and ADHD girls do not relive the experiences that I have. I want them to know that being neurodivergent means 'different, not less' and that they have incredible and valuable skills that the world needs.

And so, I stepped out as The Autistic Joyologist. Before diving into the entrepreneurial world, I spent many years in legal corporate management after graduating in Law in

2000. As I write this book, I'm celebrating over a decade as a successful entrepreneur.

The steps I took to change my life have become my RADIATE model. I knew I wanted to share my transformation with other women like me. I want to empower you to create an aligned and happy life on your terms so you can step away from the societal pressure to be 'normal'. You can stop trying to fit in, stop living on other people's terms and, instead, create a life you love. I want to show you how to do that confidently and without apology.

Recently, the BBC invited me to join Naga Munchetty's BBC 5 Live radio show to discuss autistic burnout.

Discussing my career–ending autistic burnout was a boundary I had barely brushed against in my writings, let alone openly talked about. I wasn't sure if I was ready to go there, live on air. Yet, in a whirlwind of ADHD–driven impulsivity, I found myself typing out a response, agreeing with a sense of 'delight' I wasn't sure I felt.

On the day of the interview, I sat facing my computer, joining the studio over Zoom. I could feel and hear my heart pounding during the soundcheck. I was surrounded by Post-it notes with scribbled prompts, they were my lifeline in case my thoughts decided to scatter or my brain froze.

The opening discussion featured students from the UK's only school for autistic girls. Listening to these young voices share feelings of anxiety, of being misunderstood, and their fear of being themselves with their friends struck a chord deep within me. I was transported back in time for a moment to the experiences of my younger self.

When Naga introduced a guest from The Autistic Girls Network, the conversation turned to the staggering statistic that 70–80% of autistic children are bullied. I muted my microphone to hide my reaction. The information hit too close to home. My eyes burned and a hot sensation ran through my body. History was repeating itself.

As Naga introduced me, I had to gather myself. She invited me to share my story of autistic burnout. It was time to tell the raw, unfiltered truth about the burnout that had prematurely ended my corporate career at the age of thirty–six. I even shared the moment I thought about driving my car off the road on the way home from work just to make it all go away.

I spoke about how I lost the ability to function and the immense mental, physical and emotional burnout that stripped me of my ability to carry out many daily tasks. I discussed the invisible effort I expended to make sure nobody saw my struggles and the exhaustion that masking and camouflaging caused every day. I divulged the painful moment when I knew I had to get out and the life–or–death urgency that ran through every part of me. I confessed my deep-seated shame and feeling of being 'rubbish at adulting' and the pervasive belief that I was somehow fundamentally flawed and a failure.

I shared that at the time of my burnout, I was unaware I was autistic and had ADHD. It was a diagnosis that came in my mid-forties after I had embraced entrepreneurial life – a journey that, until my diagnosis, was still shadowed by episodes of chronic burnout.

Discovering my neurodivergence, my 'AuDHD', was a turning point. I shared with Naga, and through her, with the audience, how this understanding brought about a profound shift in my life. It offered a new perspective and a chance to create a life with more balance and happiness, one where I redefined my version of success.

Naga's question about managing burnout led me to talk about the importance of recognising early signs of overwhelm and the critical need for accessible support to prevent burnout before it begins. For that, we need a great deal of self–awareness and understanding.

We need to know how to live in a way that allows us to harness skills and attributes that come naturally to us, that bring us joy and fill us with enthusiasm and energy. We must deeply understand our challenges without judgement and create supportive environments where we thrive. We need to believe we are good enough, smart enough and worthy of the life we want to live.

My story of burnout was one that was largely unseen by those around me. The chaos it wrought in my life – from the meltdowns to the sleepless nights, from the disarray at home to the overwhelming sensory inputs – remained hidden, a silent struggle.

The response to the show was overwhelming. The next day, an email from BBC 5 Live shared with me the show's significant impact. Many women resonated with my story, and others gained insights into the experiences of autistic females in their lives.

Since my diagnosis, I have known there were many out there who, like me, had constructed lives that ticked all the societal boxes for success but with immense personal consequences. Others who longed for something more, something better. The response from the show showed me that there was a greater need for a new way forward.

With The Autistic Joyologist, my intention has always been clear: to reach out to other women like me – those of us who found our neurodivergence later in life, those of us who have always felt 'different' without understanding why, and the 'neuro curious' who see a piece of themselves in stories like mine and are wondering if they, too, might be neurodivergent.

For too long, we have allowed society and others to define how we should live. We live like chameleons, hiding our true selves to try and fit in or to be 'good enough'.

Permission To Be Different is about permitting yourself to live your life in a way that feels good for you.

Take back your power and curate a life that fills every part of you with happiness, joy and a sense of achievement; a life where you are unapologetically you.

Through living this life, you are showing others what is possible for them. You are shaping the future for generations and breaking down stereotypes and stigmas associated with being neurodivergent. It's a beautiful ripple effect that will change the lives and experiences of many neurodivergent women.

You are part of a movement towards creating a more understanding and accepting society where being different is not less, where being different is celebrated.

First, you must give yourself permission to be different.

Nikki x

MY BIG PROMISE

"There are no prizes for doing life in hard mode"

— Unknown

My purpose in this book is to share a wealth of knowledge and experience to help you move from a life of overwhelm, burnout and chaos to a life where balance, joy and achievement coexist.

It will give you practical guidance and tools, along with the confidence to make the necessary changes to create the life you want. I want you to know how to make choices and decisions that support you and ensure you continue to live a life that feels successful and happy, for the long term.

I will share with you a breakdown of some of the key points I will cover throughout this book so you can decide whether you are committed to creating a life of balance, happiness and achievement right now.

My one big promise to you: stick with me through the chapters of this book, embrace the tasks I've laid out and, in just a few months, you'll see a significant shift. You will have moved away from a life of overwhelm and burnout and towards a life of balance, joy and achievement, where you enjoy all aspects of your life.

You'll find freedom in your choices and develop a loving acceptance for all you are. I will show you how, when used correctly, your core values can become your internal compass and guide your choices and decisions to ensure you create and, more importantly, sustain the life you want.

Being clear about your values and knowing how to use them as your internal compass has more power than most realise. Values are frequently spoken about, but rarely at their deepest level or in ways that enable you to absorb them into your body and mind.

Once you have mastered how to live by your values subconsciously, you will always be in alignment.

My values were not my internal compass until after my AuDHD diagnosis in my forties.

I come from a generation where we were guided to pick a career and stick to it. So, that is what I did. I followed the rules and did what was expected of me. I obeyed the 'shoulds'. After I graduated, I had a legal career and spent almost a decade leading teams. The truth is, I never enjoyed law.

I spent a decade in legal management after I chose not to qualify as a solicitor. After several years leading teams in private practice, I moved to a large corporate organisation. That leap ended with a massive burnout at thirty–six. I knew I couldn't go back to corporate life. A year after my burnout, I started on my entrepreneurial journey.

Starting my own business wasn't smooth sailing. I tried turning hobbies into businesses but it quickly took the fun out of them, so I shut them down. In 2016, I found the right fit – a niche that kept me interested because it constantly changed. It also had a profound impact on the lives of others, which gave me a sense of purpose. It did well, and I won multiple awards, but that success hid the real struggle.

The struggles were silent, invisible to everyone around me. I was doing everything alone, too frightened to ask for help in case it exposed my perceived failings. As the business grew, so did the chaos and the feeling that everything would come crashing down around me.

I know how it feels to live in constant overwhelm and burnout, to live with the consequences of being a prolific people pleaser, always falling short of the impossibly high expectations I placed on myself. I know how it feels to have the sense of never fitting in, never belonging and constantly feeling misunderstood. I know the familiar feeling of shame, of believing I wasn't good enough.

Creating a calm, fulfilling, and balanced life for myself has been the ultimate act of self–care and self–respect. I went from a life of overwhelm, unhappiness and burnout to one that feels balanced, fulfilling and happy.

I've had fantastic support since stepping out as The Autistic Joyologist, from insightful chats with the BBC and The Express newspaper to contributing to StartUps Magazine and multiple other publications, sharing advice, insights and stories.

As we move through the following chapters, we'll dive beyond anything I've shared so far. You'll learn the exact steps I took to turn my life from chaos and overwhelm to one where I have a sense of achievement, balance and joy. One which I maintain with ease these days.

In this book, I share my secrets so that you can do the same and live on your terms without constant compromise and sacrifice. *You are different, not less.*

Here's what we'll cover

To ensure we are on the same page, we will start with an overview of the terminology used throughout the chapters.

We will then look at some of the common misconceptions and beliefs about autism and ADHD that may be holding you back or that you may consider obstacles to moving forward. This will include potential fears you may have.

Then, we will look at my RADIATE model so that you have a clear idea of how this model works, the steps involved and how it can help you. We look at the best way to use the model and get the most out of it both now and for the long term.

We will spend a lot of time on how you can understand yourself on a deeper level and the steps to create the balance and achievement you want in your life. Specifically, we will cover:

- Present Position – Where are you right now? What's working for you and what isn't?
- Ideal Life – What is your ideal life? What does success mean for you? What brings you a sense of achievement? What makes you feel happy and fulfilled?
- Spiky Profile – You will discover your unique skill profile and be clear on your natural strengths to know where to focus your energy and where you may need support. This is not about improving perceived weaknesses; it's about leveraging your entire skill profile for balance and success.

- Framing and Reframing Strengths – You'll need to approach this section with curiosity and an open mind. You may have strengths you weren't aware of or strengths you believed to be weaknesses. Reframing is powerful!

- Self-Acceptance — Understanding and accepting all that you are without judgement is a powerful step in releasing the belief that you are supposed to be good at everything and any associated shame.

- Negative Narrative – This section will look at the impact of receiving negative feedback from an early age. This understanding will enable you to create positive internal feedback moving forward.

- Values – Your core values are the key to creating an aligned life. They are your internal guiding compass and the heart of my RADIATE model. Many people claim to have values, but few truly live by them. When you are clear on your values and how to use them, you will have a valuable tool for life.

- Your Internal Compass – As stated above, this section is at the heart of my RADIATE model. In it, you will learn how to connect with your values to make easy choices and decisions in life.

- Supportive Environments – To ensure that you aren't living life in 'hard mode'! There are no prizes for doing life the hard way! When you identify the areas in which you need support, help or adjustments, you will set yourself up for an easier and calmer life.

- Innovative Support Structures –This is where you identify what support you need to feel safe when facing challenges or difficulties. Rather than basing this on what you believe is available to you or 'allowed,' you will be identifying your own unique support requirements.

- Healthy Boundaries and People Pleasing – Living on other people's terms and meeting society's expectations is exhausting, and you don't need to do it! Creating healthy boundaries will reserve your energy and focus for where you *want* to put it rather than where you feel you *should*.

- Fear of Rejection or Judgement – These are common barriers to making changes in your life. By understanding how to manage and respond to these fears, you will be able to make the changes you want in your life with confidence.

- Advocating For Yourself – When you learn how to advocate for yourself, you will feel in control of your life, and your confidence will grow. I share different ways to do this so it's more comfortable.

- Advocating With Clarity – This is so that you can be clear on why you share your neurodivergence with someone and how to communicate clearly. We will look at how to share a diagnosis and any support needs in a way that improves your experiences and connections.

- Creating Change – You need to take action to create the life you want now and in the future.

- Staying Aligned – How to use my RADIATE model in all areas of your life, for big and small choices and decisions. I will show you how this model will always meet you where you are and can be an invaluable tool for living an aligned life where you feel balanced, happy and fulfilled.

- Your Legacy and Your Impact – Your actions now will transform your life and the lives of others. I will share how you aren't just changing your life, but you are also showing others what is possible for them. You are becoming an inspiring role model for other women and our future generations.

I created my RADIATE model when I couldn't find the answers or help in the tools and techniques everyone else was using and told me I 'should' use. I struggled with standard coaching methods and I began to believe my diagnosis had come too late to make the changes I desperately wanted and needed to make. Everything changed when I stepped away from all of this and focused internally.

I decided to become my own client and use my coaching skills, which I have over twenty years of experience using. I returned to the personal development work from a decade earlier and started from scratch. I embarked on a journey of self-discovery, approaching each reflection and learning with loving curiosity. I promised myself that I would move forward without judgement, and I invite you to do the same as we journey through these pages together.

When I had made significant changes in my life and mindset, I was desperate not to forget how I got there. More importantly, I wanted to stay with this beautiful sense of living on my terms, in a place of balance and happiness, where I had a sense of achievement and fulfilment. One day, as I looked out the window, daydreaming, the word 'RADIATE' came into my mind and I wrote down each step with absolute clarity.

Now, I use this model daily without having to think about it. It's a natural thought process inextricably linked to my core values, ever present as my guiding compass. I want that for you, too, because I know the freedom it brings.

Break free from the chains of societal expectations and self-imposed limitations. Embrace all you are, celebrate your victories and learn from the moments that challenge you.

You can create a life where balance and achievement coexist. You can leave overwhelm, burnout and chaos in the past and create the life you want to live – one that brings you joy, calm and fulfilment on your terms.

Are you ready? Let's get started!

1

LET'S GET ON THE SAME PAGE

Before we delve into the RADIATE model, let's make sure we are on the same page.

In this chapter, we'll look at some of the terminology that I use throughout the book and what I mean by it. You may have different interpretations to me, which is fine, but it's important to clarify what I mean, so we're not talking at cross purposes on our journey together.

We'll also touch on issues with the current outdated stereotypes, the impact they can have and why it's so important to ditch the checklists, stereotypes and labels. Only then can we live in a way that feels right for us and within a society that is open-minded, understanding and accepting of each of us, as the unique individuals we are – a society where we can stand out and stop trying to fit in, through compromise and sacrifice.

I'll also share an overview of my RADIATE model and how you can benefit from it.

First, let's start with two phrases regularly thrown at us, as neurodivergent women.

"YOU DON'T LOOK AUTISTIC"

Autism does not have a look. Comments like this highlight how outdated these stereotypes are and how society still believes them. It is also a reason why so many women don't realise they are neurodivergent until later in life, if at all.

We all have our own unique experiences and each of those experiences is entirely valid and real. Now, if someone tells me that I don't *look* autistic, I politely remind them that my autism has nothing to do with how they experience me, and everything to do with how I experience life. I invite them to open their eyes and minds, to stop believing in outdated stereotypes, to understand and accept my experiences and believe them to be true, even if I don't match the version of autism they have in their mind.

"YOU DON'T SEEM LIKE YOU'VE GOT ADHD"

I'll hold my hands up here, when someone first suggested I had ADHD, I immediately conjured up an image of a small boy running around with boundless energy, fidgeting and unable to sit still and I thought, nope – that is not me! I was guilty of buying into the stereotypes because, at that point, I didn't know any better.

There are different types of ADHD that present differently in each of us. For many women, ADHD is more internal and it's not obvious to the outside world. We can also be the masters of camouflaging and concealing the parts of ourselves we want to hide in order to be accepted and fit in. It's for these reasons, that so many females are either misdiagnosed, diagnosed much later in life, or missed altogether.

ADHD is incredibly complex and multi-faceted. If you are ADHD or have someone in your life who is, I highly recommend you check out @ADHD_Love on social media. Rich and Roxy offer amazing insights and advice as a couple where Roxy has ADHD and Rich does all he can to support her. I'm officially addicted!

WHY STEREOTYPES ARE DANGEROUS AND DAMAGING

These outdated stereotypes around autism and ADHD have a negative impact on us, as neurodivergent women, and on the way society understands and views us. The studies, research and diagnostic criteria for autism and ADHD are based on young boys – young white boys, to be precise. Even in studies that included girls, the ratio of participants was heavily male-biased.

Stereotypes around autism and ADHD also feed the narrative that we are less capable, less intelligent and, well, simply *less*, which is far from the truth.

Yes, autism and ADHD *can* be extremely limiting for some people, but not for everyone. There is a spectrum, which means every one of us has unique experiences.

The reality is that autism and ADHD often bring incredible strengths and extraordinary talents. We are different, *not* less. Stereotypes can be limiting for the individual who falls into a societal stereotype. We can start to believe the limitations placed on us, even if they aren't true.[1] There are

____

1. https://www.sciencedaily.com/releases/2015/03/150326162600.htm

multiple studies, which demonstrate this. One of the most famous was a study of women who overheard before their maths exam that females were worse than men at maths.[2] In a split test, the women who overheard this performed worse in the exam than the women who did not hear this. It's been repeated multiple times and the evidence remains the same.

To buy into stereotypes is to buy into the belief that we are all the same. Nothing could be further from the truth.

Society needs to ditch the versions of what autism and ADHD are and 'look' like and start to listen to and believe the individual lived experiences… *our* experiences. The truth is we are all unique. We will have our own experiences and they will be influenced by a myriad of factors, including (but not limited to) our childhood, upbringing, socioeconomic background, our environments, life events and trauma. They will be impacted by the people in our lives and how others treat us, good and bad.

Be proud of who you are, the real you – the brilliant you with a unique way of seeing the world and the extraordinary you who can achieve incredible things when you stop trying to fit in and start standing out. I'm excited for you to discover how amazing you truly are as we go on this journey together.

MISDIAGNOSIS MAYHEM

If ever there was evidence of the dangers of stereotypes, misdiagnosis is the ultimate red flag. Research from Durham University showed that up to 80% of autistic females were misdiagnosed, often with conditions such as anxiety, depres-

---

2. https://www.sciencedaily.com/releases/2015/03/150326162600.htm

sion, bipolar, split personality disorder and other mental health conditions. What's worse, many will likely have received medication for conditions they did not have.

I'm speaking from experience, having received a diagnosis of General Anxiety Disorder in my teens. I knew, at my core, that there was nothing general about my anxiety. What I experienced were episodes of autistic and ADHD burnout, which might look like anxiety or depression to the outside world but is a very different lived experience. My anxiety was due to living in a constant state of high alert and expending an incredible amount of effort and energy trying to fit into a society not designed for me.

Whilst there can be a co-existence of mental health conditions alongside autism and ADHD, they are often a symptom of struggling to fit into a world not designed for us rather than a standalone condition.

Had there been a greater understanding of autism and ADHD in females, and had the medical professionals looked a little closer, they would have seen an abundance of evidence that I was autistic and had ADHD as a child in school reports and discussions with my mum, as I reflected post-diagnosis.

WHAT DOES NEURODIVERSITY MEAN?

You may have heard the terms neurodiversity or neurodivergent used and have your own understanding of what these mean for you. For the context of this book, these are the definitions and interpretations used.

Neurodiversity means the variation found in people's brain function within the whole population. It includes everyone.

Every species has diversity. It's necessary for survival to adapt to changing conditions and environments. Everyone is unique in some way, yet somewhere along the line, society defined what was considered 'normal' and acceptable and built our environments and structures in a way that does not embrace neurodivergent brains.

WHAT DOES NEURODIVERGENT MEAN?

Neurodivergent refers to those whose brains function, learn and process information differently from what society expects and considers 'normal'. It includes autism and ADHD, alongside other conditions where the brain is considered to diverge from the 'norm'.

The result of this is that those of us with neurodivergent minds are often considered less in many ways, which is far from the truth. Worse still, we are forced to live in a society that does not support us, which requires immense effort and self-sacrifice. We are forced to do life in 'hard' mode.

Your neurodivergent mind is different, not less, and, in many ways, invaluable to the survival of *our* species.

Neurodivergent minds are often behind the most incredible creations, innovations and changes in our world – think Greta Thunberg and Sir Richard Branson.

Greta's unique neurodivergent perspective, intense focus and deep passion have challenged and changed societal understanding and behaviours towards climate change. Her unique approach to communication and activism highlights the strength of embracing a different way of thinking and interacting with the world.

Sir Richard Branson's entrepreneurial journey showcases how neurodivergence, with its ability to see possibilities where others see barriers, has been crucial to his innovative successes. He hasn't let his neurodivergence hold him back; instead, it fuelled a creative problem-solving approach that has driven the growth of the Virgin Group, showing that thinking differently can be the key to great success in business.

WHAT IS NEUROTYPICAL?

Neurotypical refers to people whose brains function in a similar way to most of their peers and who have behaviours and processing considered standard or typical. I use it in these pages to reference those who are not autistic or don't have ADHD and experience life in a way that conforms to societal expectations. Their minds do not diverge from what is considered acceptable or 'normal'.

'Normal' is an inappropriate word because we all have our version of what normal is for us, but it is a term often used in society instead of 'neurotypical'. I will use 'neurotypical' throughout these pages.

I believe that there are far more neurodivergent minds out there than we are currently aware of when we consider those who are undiagnosed or misdiagnosed. I suspect the ratio of neurodivergent to neurotypical isn't as wide as we might be led to believe.

DITCH THE CHECKLISTS

Forget the checklists for autism and ADHD. They are predominantly based on young boys, white middle-and-upper-class boys, to be precise. Even in more recent studies where females were included, there remained a gender bias of around 4:1 in favour of males.

Checklists confused me when I was going through diagnosis and in the following months. I compared myself to these checklists, noting where I ticked the boxes and where I didn't. For example, with my ADHD, I *do* struggle with focus, organisation, time blindness, emotional dysregulation, executive functioning and sensory overwhelm, but I *don't* constantly fidget or have a hot temper. Being autistic, I *do* have rigid routines, repetitive behaviours and struggle with social interactions, but I *don't* speak in a monotone voice, have strong special interests, and I'm no maths or coding genius! I initially questioned my diagnosis and became more confused by my own experiences because I wasn't ticking *all* the boxes.

Only when I ditched the checklists and started to pay attention to my unique experiences did I finally start to understand and accept myself exactly as I am. Letting go of the box-checking, labels, medicalisation and narrow definitions that were used to define whether I was autistic or ADHD was the best thing I could have done for myself.

Instead, focusing on deeply understanding yourself and radical self-acceptance will enable you to create a fulfilling and happy life for yourself and on your terms. You'll stop trying to fit in and conform to societal expectations and be proud to stand out as your authentic self. So, please join me in ditching these ridiculous checklists. Rip the labels off the damn boxes and get to know the real you. What really counts are *your* experiences.

THE RADIATE MODEL

Here's something I'd love you to know about tools and techniques often held up as solutions for autistic and ADHD folk – they are designed to help you work in a more neurotypical way. Whilst you may be able to do this for a short time, it's destined for failure in the long term. Your brain will never be neurotypical, no matter how hard you try and force it to be. The key to success, in my opinion, is learning how to work with your incredible brain in a way that works for you.

The RADIATE model came out of my own journey to self-understanding and acceptance after I failed miserably to find a way forward in the months after my autism and ADHD diagnosis. I'd worked with coaches and tried out multiple tools and techniques that didn't work for me, at least not in the long term.

When it comes to tools and techniques offered to help you, I invite you to think of them as hats. Try them on to see if they are a good fit and if they suit you. If they do, great! Keep them. If not, take them off and try something different. It's important to recognise when it's not working for you and step away, otherwise, you could be left feeling frustrated, hopeless and as if you are beyond help – which is exactly how I felt many times.

You can easily find that you have inadvertently created a new rule for yourself that is unhelpful because it forces you to persevere with a tool that isn't working.

The RADIATE model is not a set of tools, apps and techniques and is not a one-size-fits-all model. RADIATE is designed to meet you exactly where you are, at any point in your life, and give you a structure and framework to help you stay aligned with your values, passions, goals and dreams. It enables you to harness and maximise your unique talents and skills whilst empowering you to create a supportive environment that allows you to thrive. It will enable you to create a life where balance and achievement coexist.

The bonus is that in following RADIATE, you not only transform your life but also become an inspiring role model for others, showing them what's possible and eradicating outdated stereotypes. This, in turn, will create a more inclusive and understanding society for generations to come. Together, we are part of a movement, a powerful catalyst for change, challenging and changing the narrative around what being a neurodivergent female truly means.

Here's an overview of my **RADIATE** model:

R is for **Reflection**, which means understanding your life experiences to the present moment.

A is for **Acceptance**: to accept all your attributes without judgement.

D is for **Discovering** your core values and using them as your internal compass, to create an aligned life.

I is for **Innovate**: finding creative ways to set your life up to support you and implementing them.

A is for **Advocating** for yourself and setting healthy boundaries.

T is for **Transforming** your life and bringing it all together.

E is for **Empowering** yourself and others and being an inspiring role model.

HOW THE RADIATE MODEL WORKS

Full disclosure: RADIATE is not a quick-fix, fast-paced model. It's not something you can rattle through in a weekend by locking yourself in a room and reading this book! It's not a magic wand; you can't just read it and expect magic to happen!

NEWSFLASH

You have to commit to the exercises and take action.

The power in the RADIATE model is in building on each step in order. You'll need to take the time to reflect on your experiences, be radically honest with yourself, and commit to getting to know your true self, exactly as you are right now.

The RADIATE model requires you to take your time and commit to the process. Each step builds on the next, so work through it in the order that it's presented to you and resist the urge to skip ahead. For those of you who tend to devour information at the speed of light (hello, also me!), you might like to read through the book once, then revisit it and slowly work through each step.

RADIATE can be applied in many ways to your life. The more you use it, the easier it will become. It will *always* meet you exactly where you're at and you'll learn to tune into the steps instinctively. I found that the first time I went through RADIATE was the hardest, as it required deep reflection, honesty, courage and self-acceptance. I felt that I was learning about a whole new person, which was both terrifying and exciting at the same time.

You can choose to apply RADIATE to your whole life from the outset. Or, if you'd prefer, you can focus on a specific area, such as your work/career, personal relationships/home life or friendships/social life, for example. You can even use it for specific situations, such as a difficult work relationship or a challenging friendship. The beauty of the RADIATE model is that it always brings you back to connecting with yourself, so you will make aligned decisions that feel good for you.

GETTING THE MOST OUT OF RADIATE

To get the most out of the RADIATE model, I recommend you do these key things.

- Go through each step in order, as each builds on the previous one. Skipping steps will mean you may miss something crucial.

- Take time to go through the reflection exercises. These exercises are vital to enable you to understand your experiences. I recommend keeping notes in whichever form feels good for you – for example, a journal, notepad, notes or voice notes on your phone – as you're likely to have thoughts and feelings that pop into your head as you go about your days.

- Let go of the belief that you need to find ways to be more 'normal' or behave in a neurotypical way and focus on truly understanding and accepting yourself. You are perfect exactly as you are; you do not need to find ways to be more 'normal', only to find ways to confidently be your true self. Resist the urge to fit in and be proud to stand out.

- Understand that no one size fits all, which is why you won't find a list of tools, apps and techniques that you 'must' use. You will have the skills to identify your own needs.

- Use it as a 'rinse-and-repeat' model. It's designed to be used repeatedly throughout your life, from overhauling your whole life to dealing with daily situations and everything in between. Your life is going to change and your experiences are not static. Remember that you can use the RADIATE model repeatedly, trusting it will always meet you where you're at.

THE HAPPINESS & SUCCESS QUIZ

Take my Happiness & Success Quiz, which can be completed in less than four minutes and will give you helpful insights into where you are right now. I'd also recommend you take it again around three months after you've been through the RADIATE model for the first time.

https://quiz.autisticjoyologist.co.uk/joy

BE YOURSELF… NO, NOT LIKE THAT

I was diagnosed as autistic ADHD in my mid-forties and my world simultaneously made sense and fell apart at the same time. I had an explanation for all the challenges I'd experienced throughout my life, which felt like such a relief. At the same time, I felt a rising panic that my diagnosis had come too late.

I had already left corporate life behind over 10 years earlier, after what I now know to have been a massive autistic and ADHD burnout, which ended my corporate career at thirty-six.

I was running a specialist skin and scar clinic when I received my diagnosis. The trouble was that I could see how my business worked against me and kept me in a constant state of overwhelm, causing episodes of burnout. I desperately wanted to find a way to improve my life, but nothing seemed to work.

I hit another hurdle. As I tried to share my diagnosis with people in my life, I was met with rejection and judgement from multiple angles. Apparently, I didn't 'look' autistic, and I didn't seem like I was ADHD and 'if' I was either, I clearly wasn't that bad.

These comments and the treatment I received from those that I expected to support me stopped me in my tracks. I felt rejected, invalidated and isolated on a whole new level. I tried to be open and share the 'real' me, but I had doors slammed in my face. I wasn't 'normal' enough to fit into society, but I wasn't autistic or ADHD enough to fit into those carefully labelled boxes either.

I felt like I was living on the edge of society, living a life that crushed me with no way out. I saw memes and quotes with "Be Yourself" everywhere, but when I tried, it felt like society was telling me, "No, not like that". I felt a deep sadness, desperation and confusion, fearful I would never fit in anywhere.

I worked with coaches and followed their advice. I used the tools and techniques that were supposed to help me, but they added to my stress and anxiety because it took so much effort to try and make them work for me. I told myself I needed to try harder, but nothing stuck no matter how hard I tried. In the end, I couldn't keep up with the new habits. I desperately wanted my brain to function in the 'right' way.

That's until I realised that I didn't want that at all, that it was *impossible* to change my neurodivergent brain and that even if I could, I didn't want to! This was a huge turning point.

The tools and techniques I had been trying to use were designed to make me act in a more neurotypical way and that was an impossibility. This was a eureka moment. The moment I accepted my brain was never going to *change*, I stopped trying to change it. Instead, I focused on understanding and accepting its uniqueness and, as it turns out, pure brilliance.

I started looking inward, rather than outward, for answers and solutions. I drew on over a decade of coaching and mentoring from my corporate management career, a decade-plus of personal development work, and over a decade of entrepreneurship and mentoring. And then the magic happened.

Through genuinely understanding my unique neurodivergent brain and self, I was able to make the changes that I needed to make. I learnt to celebrate my extraordinary talents and skills and started to harness and maximise them. I became aware of my challenges and found ways to structure my life to limit their impact and to confidently advocate for my needs, unapologetically.

It was like the weight of the world had been lifted off my shoulders! The more I began to understand and accept myself, the more excited I became for my future, and my confidence grew. I went from living my life in a state of high anxiety, panic and overwhelm to being the calmest and happiest I have ever been. I began to thrive in all areas of my life and created and followed my own version of success.

To hold onto this new life and the feelings of calm and fulfilment that came with it, I developed the RADIATE model. What I love about it is that I can use it whenever I like. I can whip through the stages in minutes when I use it for something small. Sometimes, I'll address bigger areas of my life, which takes a little more time and patience, but it always works. RADIATE keeps me aligned with my true self and helps me lead the best version of my life on my terms, not everyone else's, and that's what I want for you, too.

I want you to feel confident, proud, bold, and unapologetic as you share your extraordinary self with the world. Remember, someone, somewhere, is inspired by you. They are watching you from near or afar and, through your actions, you will show them what's possible and give them permission to be their true selves, too.

SUMMARY

We've covered the terminology, touched on the dangers and challenges of stereotypes and we've looked at the RADIATE model and how to get the most from it.

Now that we are on the same page, we can enter the exciting journey of transforming your life. I ask you to approach this with an open mind and heart and to lean into each of the steps, even if they feel a little (or a lot) uncomfortable for you.

You can create a life on your terms, where you feel fulfilled, happy, supported and successful. You can learn to stand out and stop trying to fit in. You can live a bold and unapologetic life. These things are possible for you and I will show you how. Please trust in the process and know that if you follow the steps of RADIATE and immerse yourself in the journey, you *will* transform your life.

TOP FIVE TAKE-AWAYS

1. Autism and ADHD do not have a 'look'. You are unique and your experiences do not have to fit into a societal checklist or box.

2. Stereotypes are outdated and limiting. Focus on understanding and accepting yourself exactly as you are, with no judgement.

3. Neurodivergent, for the context of this book, refers to those who are autistic or ADHD, although they may have other co-existing traits or conditions.

4. Neurotypical, for the purpose of this book, refers to those who are not autistic/ do not have ADHD, and do not have neurodivergent traits or conditions.

5. The RADIATE model is here to help you live your best possible life without imposing rigid rules, tools and techniques on you.

2

REFLECTION AND PRESENT STATE

The first step of the RADIATE model is Reflect. Reflection can be difficult and uncomfortable sometimes. Reflections, or 'a-ha' moments, often come when you least expect them, so I recommend having a notebook to hand or making notes on your phone when you have spontaneous thoughts. Take your time with this chapter; it is the foundation for the rest of the RADIATE model.

Here, you'll also consider what your ideal life looks like and what success means for you. Don't be surprised if you feel some resistance. Many of us have spent our lives as prolific people pleasers and will naturally think about what we are 'allowed' to do. I invite you to move past the beliefs of what you might feel you're allowed and to think about what you want for your life and what success and happiness look like.

I will ask you to imagine your ideal life in as much glorious detail as possible.

By the end of this chapter, you will have a clear idea of where you are in your life right now and a vision for your ideal life that excites you. Get ready to start the transformation process – there's no going back now!

WHERE ARE YOU RIGHT NOW?

Trigger warning: Reflection can bring discomfort and can be triggering. It's essential that this is a positive experience for you, so please don't force yourself to continue if you feel triggered. You can return to it when you feel ready. If you feel that you need support, I recommend that you work with a trained professional therapist or coach, or, at the very least, have the support of someone you trust.

Answer the questions below to get started. You might need to come back to them, as we often resist our true feelings at first glance. There are no right or wrong answers and your first answer doesn't have to be your last. You might return to a question at another time and have a different perspective then.

You need to deeply understand where you are today so that you can reflect on what has worked for you up to this point, what hasn't, and why. This is how you will honour your needs while you showcase your talents to create balance, happiness and fulfilment in your life.

I'd like you to consider three areas of your life. Reflect on your current experiences, feelings and thoughts around these areas. Brainstorm and get as much out of your head as possible. If focusing on all areas at once feels overwhelming, please pick one.

Work/Career:

- What is your professional life currently like for you?
- How does the work you do impact you?
- How many hours are you working?
- What is your work environment like?
- How do you feel about work?
- Do you enjoy your work, the environment and the people?

Personal Life/Relationships:

- What is your personal life currently like for you?
- Are you married, single, with/without children?
- Do you live alone, with friends, or with family?
- What are your close personal relationships like?
- How do you feel about your current circumstances?
- What emotions do you feel about your personal life?
- Do you feel supported, happy, calm? Or lonely, isolated, or misunderstood?

Social Life and Friendships:

- What is your social life currently like for you?
- Do you have a large group or a couple of close friends, or spend much of your time alone?
- Do you go out or prefer to stay in?
- Are you happy with your social life and friendships?
- What are your favourite things to do socially?
- What do you dislike doing?

If you'd like to do this for other areas of your life, then apply the same questions.

Now that you know where you are in key areas of your life, we will do something that might feel uncomfortable and scary. Sometimes, when we face the truth about our lives, it can be painful. It can feel impossible to imagine a life that is one that we choose on our terms, but you *can* do this, I believe in you! Please sit with it and know that on the other side is a life that will feel more balanced and aligned with how you want to live.

WHAT'S WORKING AND WHAT ISN'T?

In each area you've reflected on, think about what's working for you and what isn't and then think about why. Reflecting on this is powerful as it will help you to see where you can make changes to enhance your experiences and areas of your life.

Here are some examples to help.

Work: You might love your work and find it plays to your natural strengths and talents; however, you might constantly feel overwhelmed and overstimulated by the end of the day. If you reflect on what works and what doesn't, you might discover that you enjoy your work but struggle with the environment or work volume.

Personal: You may love your partner/children but feel that you take on all the responsibilities in the household and find it overwhelms you, especially alongside your work commitments. You never feel like you have time to relax and switch off, and you wish there were days when you could escape the pressure.

Friendships and Socialising: You may be part of a social group where one or more of your friends demands much of your time or energy. Perhaps they are only there when they need you and never support you. You may feel like you're the one making all the effort, but you don't know how to say no, as you're worried that they will think you don't care and won't want to be your friend anymore.

In all the areas of your life that you've chosen to reflect on, think about what you like and what works for you, then think about what you don't like and doesn't work for you. Write your reflections on two separate lists.

Think about the why, too. This will help you to see whether there are any common themes or patterns.

Before we move on, I want to mention people-pleasing and fear of rejection. These gremlins can show up and make you believe you can't move forward or make changes in your life. If they show up for you and create resistance, and you push through that resistance, it will be worth it in the long run.

OVERDELIVERING, PEOPLE-PLEASING AND PERFECTIONISM

After a period of reflection, it is common to feel some discomfort and unease. Rarely do we give ourselves permission to be this honest about how we feel.

Maybe you've spent most of your life as a prolific people-pleaser, hoping you'll fit in and be accepted by others. Perhaps you've been so painfully aware of what you perceived as your shortcomings that you consistently over-deliver to look as though you have it all together and are competent.

If this sounds like you, your focus will have been on the needs and wants of others. As a people-pleaser, it's easy to ignore your wants because you believe they are not as important as everyone else's. I spent my life living in fear that others would find out I didn't know what I was doing, worried I'd be found out and rejected, dismissed, and thought of as incompetent or worthless. Overdelivering was a default setting, with the belief that nothing I did was good enough. Saying yes to everyone's demands, no matter the personal consequence. If this is you, I feel your pain and I'm sending you a massive virtual hug. Please understand that your needs and wants are valid and essential for living a life in balance, and you are perfect as you are.

FEAR OF REJECTION AND NOT BEING GOOD ENOUGH

This sums up how I have felt most of my life. If you've spent much of your life trying to keep everyone else happy, then the chances are that you feel the same way, too.

Fear of rejection can be a powerful and emotive driver to try and keep others happy while you compromise and sacrifice your needs and feelings. Over time, this builds up and your focus centres wholly on the needs of others, leaving you feeling anxious, overwhelmed, on high alert and, frankly, exhausted.

Have you heard of Rejection Sensitive Dysphoria (RSD)? It's common amongst autistic and ADHD women. RSD is an often-overlooked emotional response to *perceived* criticism, rejection, failures or judgement that causes intense emotional pain. The keyword here is 'perceived'.

Throw in the sensory sensitivities and social challenges many of us experience, and you have a recipe for a lifetime of angst and overwhelm. This potent fear of rejection or perception of not meeting expectations can make you dread even the slightest negative evaluation. This leads to a life filled with hesitation, self-doubt, and an agonising quest for perfection.

The topic of RSD is a book on its own, but here are five signs you might have RSD:

1. Intense emotional responses.
2. Anticipating rejection or fearing it ahead of a situation.
3. Ruminating on past events and replaying them in your mind.
4. Physical responses such as dizziness, racing heart and digestive symptoms.
5. Perfectionism.

If these signs describe you, you will need to make some changes to create the life you genuinely want to live in a way that feels good for you. You will likely have moments of fear along the way. If you understand and accept this, you can work through it. You're okay, you've got this.

PLAYING IT SMALL AND UNDERACHIEVING

I talk a lot about defining success on your own terms and creating a life of balance, happiness and achievement. Success and achievement take many forms.

Some of you might relate to this based on your educational or career accolades, but this message is equally, if not more, vital for those of you who might feel like you've somehow fallen short of your potential because of fear, challenges, or deep-seated beliefs that you weren't enough in some way.

Success isn't a defined term; it will mean something different for each of us. For some, it might mean financial stability, to others, it could mean having a rich personal life filled with love and laughter.

Your journey is uniquely yours and valid, no matter how it looks to others.

If you've ever felt that you've played it small or been held back by invisible barriers that seemed too dense to break through, know this – you are not alone. And more importantly, it's never too late to create a life that is fulfilling, where you have a sense of achievement that is meaningful for you.

Playing it small can often be a protective response – your mind shielding you from potential failure or rejection. It might have felt safer to remain in the shadows rather than step into the light and risk falling short.

These fears are real, but they don't define you. You can change the narrative, release the limiting beliefs and create the life you want to live.

While you navigate creating a life of balance, happiness and success, remember that the focus is on creating a life that feels good for *you*. It's about waking up most mornings feeling like you are exactly where you want and need to be.

Stay curious and be open to the possibilities of new experiences.

RELEASE LIMITING BELIEFS

Limiting beliefs are beliefs that hold you back and stop you from fulfilling your true potential. They are beliefs you have about yourself, or they could be beliefs about others, society or something else. The chances are, you are not even aware of many of them because they are subconscious.

Many of our beliefs are formed in childhood and are passed to us from our parents, family, culture, society, school and friends. In essence, they are not ones we have formed from experiences we have had ourselves. We also form new beliefs as we mature.

These are examples of limiting beliefs.

"It's selfish to put my needs before others."

"I never do anything right."

"Success is measured by money and status."

"I'm not good enough/smart enough."

"I don't have what it takes to succeed in business/professionally."

"If I show my true self, I will be rejected."

"If I ask for help, it shows I can't cope."

"No one values my ideas or opinions."

"I am unlovable/not worthy of love."

It is important to consider and be aware of your limiting beliefs. Take some time to reflect on the beliefs you hold and ask yourself these questions:

Q: What is the belief?

Q: Where does it come from? How did I form this belief?

Q: How does this belief impact my life? How/where is it holding me back?

Q: Is there another, more positive belief I could choose instead?

Q: How would the new belief help me?

Beliefs can be changed; they are not set in stone. They are not the same as objective facts. Objective facts can be verified, supported by evidence, and remain the same for everyone. For example, 'The sun rises in the east and sets in the west', 'Five plus four equals nine', or 'The boiling point of water is around 100 degrees Celsius'.

Beliefs *can* be changed. If you can identify the limiting belief and where it came from, you can challenge it and replace it with something which serves you better.

If you use statements such as "I can't do that," ask yourself, "But what if I can? What would that mean for me if I did?" Or, if you believe "I'm not allowed to do that," ask yourself, "Who says I'm not allowed? What would happen if I did?".

Addressing any limiting beliefs you have at this stage will enable you to choose new ones as you move forward to create the life you want to live, not one based on the beliefs that will limit your options and hold you back from reaching your full potential.

You may feel that your beliefs are integral to your identity, but they are not. Beliefs are simply thoughts, thought multiple times until they become subconsciously stored in your brain and you no longer have conscious awareness of them.

Think of your thoughts as paths you walk down repeatedly. If you travel the same path enough times, it becomes well-worn and familiar; this is how a belief forms. Once established, these beliefs act as filters, shaping how you see and interpret the world around you. They make you notice only the things that confirm what you already believe. When you recognise this, you open up to changing your route and discovering new paths.

You can choose new beliefs that are more desirable to you, which enable you to create the changes you want to make in your life.

Changing these beliefs starts with recognition. Identify a belief that no longer serves you, like, "I must do everything perfectly," and challenge it. Ask yourself, "Is this really true?" Explore the origins of this belief and assess its current impact on your life. By understanding that these are just thoughts you've repeated and not truths etched in stone, you can begin to consciously choose and reinforce new beliefs that support your aspirations and reflect your true self. Just as you evolve over the years, so, too, can your beliefs. This change isn't just possible; it's a pathway to a freer, more fulfilling life.

WHAT DOES YOUR IDEAL LIFE LOOK LIKE?

Do you lie in bed at night, wishing life could be easier?

Do you wish you could get up in the morning and look forward to your day or get into bed at night feeling you've had a great day?

What is your ideal life like? Take some time to visualise or consider your perfect day, from getting up in the morning to going to bed at night. I am *not* asking you to imagine a perfect day that is an escape from your reality, such as being on holiday. Rather, I want you to imagine a wonderful day that is your *daily reality*, one that feels balanced, fulfilling and rich in every way possible.

- What are you doing?
- Who are you with?
- Where do you find moments of joy, and what makes you smile?
- Where do you feel lit up and fulfilled?
- What emotions, thoughts or feelings do you experience?

Imagine it all in as much colour as possible. If you are not a visual thinker, write down or voice record your thoughts.

Imagine your perfect life on your terms, not based on what you think you're allowed or would be acceptable to others. This is key.

Remove all the expectations and limitations from your mind and let your imagination run wild. There are no rules. It doesn't have to feel realistic or achievable, and you don't need to figure out how to get there right now; you just need to connect to what you truly want in your life, to what's important to you, and *why*.

This is a powerful exercise. Start with this sentence and let your mind explore.

"I am living my best life right now, and it's like..."

WHAT DOES SUCCESS MEAN TO YOU?

In modern society, we are often shown that the car, house, job, possessions and fancy holidays measure success. Yes, money helps to make our lives more comfortable and can create choices, but money and status are not the benchmarks for success and happiness.

Success isn't about money, status or fame; it's about accomplishing a goal you set out to achieve. That goal is up to you.

What does a successful life look like for you? Here are some ideas that are based on something other than societal definitions of success.

- You can enjoy meals with your family every night.
- You feel calm and in control of your life.
- You feel healthy and you prioritise your well-being.
- You have time for activities that you enjoy.
- You pursue a passion or purpose that means something to you.

Think about what success means to you. Five years from now, if someone asks you how you achieved success, what story are you telling? What are your biggest successes and what makes them successful and meaningful to you?

LIVING LIFE ON YOUR TERMS

Chances are, you've never given much thought to life on your terms, as you've been too busy living on everyone else's terms. Now is the time to put your wants and needs first.

I'll tell you a secret: when I went through these steps myself, I realised I wasn't just living life on some*one* else's terms; I was living on *everyone* else's terms! I had spent over four decades expertly figuring out what was expected of me, what I was allowed to do, and how I was allowed to do it. I had become the master chameleon of being whatever version of myself I needed to be to try and fit in and be accepted.

My mind was blank when I challenged myself to think about living life on my terms. I was drawn back to what others thought was acceptable. No one had ever asked what I wanted or needed, so it was hard to ask myself and even harder to believe it was possible.

I want you to know that whatever you want or need is perfect.

 ## NEWSFLASH
Your wants and needs are valid and are essential to your well-being and enjoyment of life.

As you move through this book and the exercises, notice when your mind wanders to what you think you're allowed, or what others will accept, and bring your focus back to *your* wants and needs.

WHAT IS YOUR VISION FOR THE FUTURE?

What does your vision for the future look and feel like? Think deeply about what living a thriving, happy and successful life means for you – not just for work but all areas of your life. It doesn't matter if it is nothing like the life you currently lead, and equally, it's okay if it does resemble your current life, but perhaps with some upgrades and tweaks.

It's also okay not to know at this stage. If you find it hard to envision your future, sit with it. As you work through the RADIATE model, you'll gain the confidence and skills to help you create a vision for your future in your own time. There's no rush.

CREATING A VISION FOR YOUR FUTURE

Now that you have reflected on your ideal life, I want you to create a vision for your future. You can do this in any way you choose, as long as you create it in a way that allows you to revisit and update it regularly.

We are going to look at how to create a vision board and life story vision. They are a powerful reminder of the life you strive for. If you create a vision in a way that feels good for you, it will deeply resonate. You will find a link in the resources to a video with guidance on creating your vision board if you need it.[3] You can make notes in a journal if you'd prefer. I had a client who created their vision board as a video with music. Every time she watched it, she connected with her vision for her life, which was extremely powerful for her.

I recommend that your vision board or life story vision include all areas of your life to ensure you create a life that works harmoniously for you. This will prevent conflicting goals and dreams in different areas of your life.

Firstly, we will look at vision boards; if you'd prefer to create a life story instead, go to the exercise below this one.

---

3. https://youtu.be/6xzZjDzW3SE Creating a Vision Board

Exercise: Vision Board

Step 1: Decide whether you want to create a physical or digital board. Tools like Canva, Pinterest, or PowerPoint work perfectly for a digital board. This allows for easy updates and changes as your goals evolve.

Step 2: Take time to think deeply about all areas of your life that are important to you. This might include your career, personal growth, health, relationships, and hobbies. Reflect on what balance in these areas would be like and how they interconnect and influence or affect each other.

Step 3: Search for images and quotes that resonate with your vision and aspirations. Choose visuals that spark positive emotions and align closely with your life goals.

Step 4: Arrange your images and quotes on your board or digital canvas. Place them in a way that each life area is visually represented. For instance, you might place images relating to your professional aspirations in one section and those related to personal wellness in another. The layout should reflect the connections between these areas, showing how each contributes to your overall life balance.

Place your physical vision board in a spot where you'll see it daily. For digital boards, set it as your desktop wallpaper or keep it easily accessible on your phone or computer. Regularly viewing your board will help keep your goals fresh in your mind and motivate you to take actionable steps towards them.

Exercise: Life Story Vision; Written or Recorded

When creating your life vision story, either written or auditory, keep yourself as the lead character in your story.

Use the first person and present tense to immerse yourself in the experience. Describe each scenario as if you're living it right now: "I am confidently delivering my pitch to a new client, feeling energised and calm." Or, "I am laughing with friends over a delicious dinner, feeling a deep sense of belonging and joy."

This approach helps you vividly imagine and connect with your vision, making it feel more natural, real, desirable and achievable.

Step One: Begin by thinking about the key areas of your life as chapters in a book. These might include Career, Personal Growth, Health, Relationships, and Hobbies. Consider what you want each of these chapters to contain – what stories do you want to tell in each area?

Step Two: For each chapter, write down a detailed description of your ideal scenario. What is happening in your career or working life? What adventures do you want to experience in your personal life? Who is present in your life? How do you see your health and relationships evolving? Be as specific and vivid as you can, creating a rich narrative for each part of your life.

Step Three: Consider the goals that can turn these scenarios into reality. Make sure you include your passions and interests to ensure your life is aligned in all areas.

Step Four: Reflect on how these chapters are interconnected. How does achieving your health goals support your career ambitions? How do your relationships enrich or support your personal growth? Understanding these connections can help you prioritise and focus on actions that have multiple benefits across different areas of your life.

Step Five: Keep this document or recording accessible, whether in digital format on your device or as a printout in your workspace if it's in written format. Make it a habit to reflect on, read through or listen to your life story every week or month.

You will revisit your vision further as you progress through these pages.

A LEAP OF FAITH

When I went through the Reflection step, everything changed. I sat with discomfort, sadness and grief as I came to terms with the fact that I'd spent most of my life living on other people's terms, hiding away my true self and holding myself back from my dreams.

I decided to stop trying to fit in and I committed to knowing my neurodivergent self on a deep level.

While I was in a much better place running my clinic than I had been during my corporate days, I could see where my life was stacked against me. I had focused on what I felt I 'should' do and not what I wanted to do.

Several months after my diagnosis, I wasn't making any progress. I'd worked with coaches and used the recommended tools, but they didn't have the impact I needed. I was afraid that I'd have to accept that this was my life. Except I knew deep down that I *could* make the changes I craved; I just had to figure out how.

Following the Reflection process, I could see my fear of judgement and rejection had led me to do things others expected of me. I'd prioritised the needs and wants of others over my own and sacrificed my happiness, well-being and success. I could see where I'd constantly over-delivered and I was caught in a web of prolific people-pleasing, constantly in fear that I'd fail or let someone down. To manage the turmoil and challenges within my work environment, I'd fully retreated from having social interactions and personal relationships. I was lonely, isolated, overwhelmed and exhausted.

Then I thought about what my ideal life would look like, my perfect day. What would I be doing, where would I go and who would I be with? That perfect life didn't look much like the one I was living, but the thought of it made me smile. I felt both excited and terrified of being able to live the life I had imagined.

Here's a fun (but powerful) fact: Did you know that fear and excitement trigger a similar physiological reaction in the body? The nervousness you feel about asking for a promotion or raise is natural, but you could also see it as excitement about advancing your career. Starting a new hobby can feel daunting, but you can flip this fear into excitement about learning a new skill, connecting with like-minded people and enriching your life with new experiences. And, if public speaking makes your palms sweat and heart pound, try seeing it as a rush of excitement, an opportunity to share your passion and make an impact. When I feel fear about life events, I tell myself it's just excitement that needs an attitude adjustment! It works, try it.

I realised I'd created a life based on what others wanted, needed and expected from me, but I had ignored my wants and needs. This was like a massive lightbulb being switched on and I could see clearly for the first time.

When I created my vision board, I got lost in the possibility and excitement of it all. I'm visual, so my vision board is full of photos and quotes that deeply resonate with me. After I'd created it, I cried because I could finally see my truth and what I really wanted in my life. And I cried because it felt so far away at that moment.

It felt like sitting on the edge of a plane waiting to do a skydive – something I experienced when I was nineteen. I looked out and saw the vast expanse of the world beneath me, knowing that to get to a safe place, I first had to jump and free fall. I knew that after the freefall, the parachute would open, the descent would slow, and the feeling of safety and knowing would return until, finally, I was on safe ground again.

I just had to jump and take a leap of faith.

I knew I had taken the first step to create the changes I needed to make to support and align with my neurodivergent self. It felt powerful, magical and, above all else, possible. My vision for my life was realistic; I didn't want to live on the moon surrounded by unicorns. I wanted an entirely possible life if I was brave enough to make the changes. And I did. And the rollercoaster of emotions and uncomfortable experiences were worth it.

SUMMARY

You've been able to reflect on how you've gotten to this point in your life and the reasons behind this. You've also brought awareness to how you would like your life to look and what a successful and happy life could look like for you, on your terms.

When you have a vision for your future that excites you, you'll feel motivated to create it. Your vision might change over time, and that's okay. You can update your vision board anytime and align your life with your new vision and goals. The RADIATE model will always guide you wherever you are.

With this in mind, you are in a powerful position to move onto the next step of the RADIATE model, Accept, where we dig deeper into your strengths and discover more about the real you.

TOP FIVE TAKE-AWAYS

1. Start with a deep understanding of where you are right now to move forward with purpose.

2. Fear of rejection or judgement can lead to a life of overdelivering and people-pleasing, which can cause overwhelm and unhappiness.

3. Your wants, desires and needs are valid. You do not need permission from anyone else to live life on your terms.

4. You can create a thriving, happy and successful life on your terms (even if you don't believe that right now).

5. When you create a vision for the future that includes your whole life, it ensures you have the best version of your life, whether that's a vision board, life story, soundboard or something else. Create your vision, your way.

3

A IS FOR ACCEPT

Now that you've reflected on where you are right now, it is time to work on self-acceptance. This may feel uncomfortable but don't worry, I'll guide you through and, by the end of this chapter, you will have a deeper understanding and acceptance of your true self.

Self-acceptance is the key to maximising and harnessing your strengths in a supportive and safe environment. Understanding and accepting your true self will create a life aligned with your values, desires, goals and needs.

For our purposes here, acceptance means reaching a point where you understand yourself and accept all your attributes, positives and perceived negatives, where you release judgement and get to know all parts of yourself. This isn't a quest to turn all attributes into a positive – I'm not going to give you a load of positive mantras to chant, but if that's your thing, go for it!

Acceptance will help you let go of the belief that you're not good enough and need to change yourself to adapt to the expectations of others. You do not need to change; it's time for society to understand, accept and support you exactly as you are.

ACCEPTING AND EMBRACING YOUR 'SPIKY PROFILE'

The term 'spiky profile' refers to those of us who have big gaps in our skill sets.

Research[4] shows more significant differences in skill capability in the neurodivergent community than for neurotypicals. While every human is better at some things than others, neurotypicals tend to have more average capabilities across the board when it comes to their life skills.

If you are neurodivergent, you may notice that you excel in some areas while struggling to carry out everyday tasks that many find easy. You may be an incredibly creative writer, but you find it difficult to talk on the phone. You might easily solve complex problems, but you can't follow simple directions in the car. These big gaps in skills create spikes when you look at your overall skillset.

When you understand your unique spiky profile, you can learn to focus on maximising the areas you excel in and finding the support you need in the areas that you find more challenging.

---

4. Nancy Doyle, Neurodiversity at work: a biopsychosocial model and the impact on working adults, *British Medical Bulletin*, Volume 135, Issue 1, September 2020, Pages 108–125, https://doi.org/10.1093/bmb/ldaa021

And remember, you do NOT need to be good at everything! Richard Branson and Steven Bartlett are famous for being honest and sharing their shortcomings with specific skills. They know they don't have to be brilliant at everything; they need to recruit people who excel in the areas they don't.

If you have spent your life believing you need to try harder, do better and be better to be good at everything, then give yourself permission to let go of that belief right now.

During the reflections in this chapter, be curious about your strengths, challenges and attributes. Please get to know your unique spiky profile, understand how your skills and attributes impact your life and accept them. Release the desire to change because you'll see yourself through a new, beautiful lens once you realise your unique skills and talents are assets.

MANAGING THE CHALLENGES

We all find certain things in our lives difficult. What's important is to recognise your challenges and create a supportive environment to thrive. This is not about forcing yourself to master skills you find difficult, frustrating or downright impossible! Don't waste your energy.

In areas I find difficult, my first step is removing unnecessary pressure. When you do this, you ensure that when you consider your support needs, you focus on where you can add value to your life rather than on unnecessary areas.

I created my ADE process to help focus on this. Ask yourself these questions for each area of your life:

AUTOMATE: Can I automate a process or task that would help me in this situation?

DELEGATE: Do I need to be doing this, or can someone else do it?

ELIMINATE: Is this even necessary?

Using ADE will help you to simplify and streamline many areas of your life quickly.

Accepting your challenges and looking for ways to enhance your life is powerful and transformational. If you only bring awareness to your challenges, you're unlikely to make any meaningful changes. You need to understand and accept them as well.

# *NEWSFLASH*

You do not need anyone else's permission to make changes in your life.

USING ADE IN YOUR PROFESSIONAL AND PERSONAL LIFE

Your challenges will be different from mine. Don't worry if the exact scenario does not resonate with you. Focus on the principles instead.

Work

You feel overwhelmed and out of control. Your paperwork is building up, and you have multiple projects to focus on and meetings to attend. You have a constant fear of failure, which results in sleepless nights. You go to bed with thoughts of what you didn't manage to do that day and a sense of worry for the next day. You wake up in the morning in a state of dread and anxiety. The ADE method can help.

Automate:

- Are there parts of your work that you could automate, such as a booking system, automated reminders, repeat orders, and scheduling?
- Could you set up automatic payments, invoicing and reminders?
- Are there other areas you could automate?

Delegate:

- Could you outsource or delegate tasks or elements of tasks to someone else, whether that's an employee, a colleague, or a virtual support worker?
- If self-employed, could you outsource administration, social media, finances and ordering?
- What tasks are not a good use of your time or are not within your skill set? Could someone else help with these?

Eliminate:

- Are there tasks you are doing that you don't need to do or add no value? Sometimes, we do things out of habit, even when they offer no value. Make a list of your responsibilities and see if you can identify tasks or activities you could stop (or automate).

Personal

You are spinning many plates and fear you'll drop one (or more) any day. You live in constant fear that you'll let someone down. You feel as though you are responsible for the happiness of everyone around you. You feel exhausted, overwhelmed and underappreciated. How ADE could help:

Automate:

- Set up a weekly online supermarket shop with repeat items.
- Set up subscriptions for essential items like toilet rolls (Amazon is great for this).
- Set up direct debits and standing orders for bills to remove the worry of late payments.

Delegate:

- Ask your partner or children for help with tasks around the home or consider a cleaner.
- If you do a school run, consider whether you could ride share with another parent and take turns to do collection or drop off.

Eliminate:

- Could you batch-make meals one day a week and store them in the fridge or freezer? I love this hack; I batch cook meals because some days, I reach into the fridge or freezer to access nutritious food, so I don't have to prepare or cook anything from scratch.

DIFFERENT, NOT LESS

Understanding and accepting yourself are essential to enable you to move forward.

I felt I didn't fit in or belong my whole life. I struggled with things others found easy in every area of my life. I spent years in therapy, desperate to figure out what was wrong with me so I could fix it. I never found the answers; I felt broken, isolated and disconnected, despite my efforts.

My autism and ADHD diagnoses were the best gifts I could have received because, suddenly, it all made sense.

Shortly after diagnosis, I watched Brene Brown, the renowned shame researcher, on YouTube, where she said, "I will not negotiate who I am with you, not anymore."[5] It hit me like a thunderbolt. I knew, from that moment, that this was my new life mantra.

As I leaned into acceptance, I told myself that I am different, not less. My differences make me unique and extraordinary. I stopped apologising when there was nothing to apologise for, and I stopped being a prolific people pleaser.

Remember that you are different, not less. You are incredibly talented and gifted, and you deserve to shine and have a successful and happy life.

RELEASE THE DESIRE TO BE NORMAL

What does 'normal' even mean? Even if 'normal' existed, who wants to be that? It's like only eating vanilla ice cream for the rest of your life, with no sprinkles or toppings.

Release the desire to behave in a neurotypical way. Don't try to act and think like a neurotypical because it won't work. This is where many coaching methods, tools and techniques get it wrong. They are geared to make us act in a more neurotypical way, which sets us up for failure.

Where are my planner and diary collectors? I see you! I counted mine for this book. I have sixty-two different versions of time planners, diaries and notebooks designed to help me meticulously plan my days and week. The most

---

5. https://youtu.be/EI89XK2L6I4

I've ever sustained a new time management system for is ten days, thanks to my autistic need for order and routine, coupled with my ADHD ability to hyper-fixate on new things. New time management approach, new notebook. I couldn't use the one I already had because that one hadn't worked and, clearly, the failure was down to the planner, not the fact that I forced my brain to act in a way it couldn't.

The effort and energy it takes to force your brain to work unnaturally will exhaust you. When it doesn't work (and it most likely won't in the long term), you'll believe that the fault is in you and you're beyond help. This is not true.

Once you can understand and accept how your unique brain works, you can set your life up to work for you and release what doesn't work. You can only do this if you're committed to letting go of the desire to be neurotypical and embrace your incredible neurodiverse mind.

ACCEPT YOURSELF AS YOU ARE IN THE MOMENT

Have you found that your experiences fluctuate? Maybe you struggled with a situation or task on one day but excelled at it on another. Your experiences will not be static; they will change throughout your life. You may recall times when you have felt calm, happy and in control. Other times may have been more of a challenge or resulted in burnout, shutdown or meltdown.

Reflecting on different times of your life and your experiences can help highlight common themes or patterns.

However, always meet yourself where you are at any given moment. Release any judgement you may feel about not being consistent in how you think or act. And, please, stop telling yourself to do better or try harder.

Many factors can impact how you feel and your ability to cope and function. Sleep, stress, nutrition, health, environment and life circumstances all play a part. Ask yourself, "What do I need right now?" when you feel overwhelmed or anxious. Box breathing is a powerful way to calm your nervous system and settle your mind. Ten to fifteen rounds of box breathing can be transformational. Try it the next time you feel anxious or overwhelmed and see how you get on.

Box Breathing Technique: Breathe in for a count of four, hold your breath for a count of four, breathe out for a count of four, and hold for a count of four. Repeat for at least ten rounds.

This breathing exercise is scientifically proven to reduce stress responses in your body. It is also a helpful tool if you struggle to switch between tasks. Taking time to do this at the end of a task before you start a new one can make the transition easier.

THE IMPORTANCE OF SELF-ACCEPTANCE

Self-acceptance is a superpower, a portal to a happy, balanced and fulfilling life.

Without it, your life will be harder than it needs to be. You will be exhausted and eventually overwhelmed when you force yourself into situations and environments that feel difficult or uncomfortable or try to act unnaturally. You will also feel disconnected and isolated as you act out a version of yourself you believe others will prefer.

The kindest thing you can do for yourself is to accept every part of you without judgement. Learn to understand your unique strengths and skills and the areas you find difficult. Accept all your attributes with kindness and learn to build a life that supports you so that you can enjoy a happy and successful life on your terms.

When it comes to being neurodivergent, you cannot change how your brilliant mind works. You can learn tools and strategies to enhance your life, but no matter how hard you try, you'll never turn your neurodivergent mind into a neurotypical one.

RADICAL HONESTY AND SELF-COMPASSION

Radical honesty means being honest with yourself about who you are. Self-compassion asks you to show kindness and understanding and stop being self-critical and judgemental.

When your inner critic kicks in, change the narrative. Release the negative self-talk, shame, criticism and judgement. Instead, offer yourself support and encouragement. When you understand and accept yourself, you will discover this comes naturally. Almost immediately after my diagnosis, much of my negative self-talk fell away and it was replaced with pride, compassion and kindness.

A great exercise is to imagine you are talking to your best friend. Think about how you would respond to them, what words and tone you would use and what support you would offer. It's a great way to experience yourself through a different lens, from a place of love and kindness.

GET CLEAR ON YOUR STRENGTHS

Your strengths are the things you are good at, that come easily to you or have mastered. Strengths are skills or attributes that you carry out with ease and often with a sense of calm competence.

When you regularly use your strengths, your confidence will grow. Research[6] has shown that when people focus on their strengths, it leads to higher life satisfaction and improves mental well-being.

Brainstorm your strengths, and if you have someone in your life whose opinion you value and who knows you well, ask them what they think, too. They may notice some you're unaware of or haven't considered before. You may uncover strengths you had forgotten about, suppressed or don't regularly use.

Write down your five top strengths. They could be technical or creative skills, or the ability to solve complex problems creatively. They could be personal skills such as leadership and empathy, or you might be a great communicator or speaker.

Now that you've chosen five strengths, are you making the most of them?

This can be an eye-opener as you reconnect with your strengths and look at where you currently use them. Also, consider where you can use them more or in different ways. If you uncover strengths you had forgotten, think about how you could start to use them and where they could enhance your life.

---

6. https://www.ncbi.nlm.nih.gov/pmc/articles/PMC3939995/

As I mapped out my vision for the future, I considered what my strengths were. I realised that some things that I had been criticised for in the past were actually strengths. My ability to see creative solutions to problems or new ways to work that had been rejected, laughed at or ignored throughout my corporate career was powerful as an entrepreneur. I hadn't let those skills shine because others had belittled them.

I suddenly saw opportunities to use my strengths in new and transformative ways. I could also see that areas that were challenging for me didn't have to be if I adapted my life and asked for help and support.

REFRAME YOUR PERCEPTION OF ATTRIBUTES

You probably have strengths that you believed were weaknesses or flaws. Or skills that you feel were not wanted or needed if they have been rejected or criticised by others.

You may have things you'd consider challenges that are a strength when harnessed and thought of differently.

Take impulsivity and risk-taking as an example. They are often considered negative attributes, such as online shopping or thrill-seeking. When you look at these attributes in the context of entrepreneurship or leadership, they could be two of your greatest strengths. Nothing would ever change in the business world without risk-taking and impulsivity, and we need change to drive innovation and growth. The Harvard Business Review reports[7] that neurodiversity is a competitive business advantage.

---

7. Neurodiversity Is a Competitive Advantage (hbr.org)

MAXIMISE YOUR STRENGTHS FOR AUTHENTICITY

Although it is an overused word today, authenticity is vital to ensure you stay connected with yourself and your values. When you maximise your strengths for authenticity, you can let them shine through without fear of how others will perceive them.

Letting your strengths shine through will make you feel fulfilled, confident and proud of your abilities. Permitting your true self to shine inspires others to be their authentic selves and stand out from the sameness we often see in business environments.

What could you achieve if you proudly let your true strengths shine through?

What would happen if you maximised your strengths, achieved your goals and dreams, and created a life where you feel fulfilled, calm and balanced? Take a moment to explore this, either through visualising and imagining yourself living this way or recording your thoughts in a way that works for you.

BE PROUD OF YOUR STRENGTHS AND TALENTS

We live in a society that celebrates sameness much of the time. Sameness is boring and achieves little other than maintaining the status quo. Our environments and experiences have, and still are, changing rapidly, and to adapt to these changes, the world needs diversity and new ways to exist as we continue to evolve.

Your brilliantly unique mind has strengths and talents that neurotypical minds do not possess. You can see things differently, which gives you the ability to create radical change in many ways you may not have considered. Your skills enable you to add value and make a difference.

Be proud of your uniqueness rather than trying to fit in with everyone else. Be proud of your valuable insights. Be proud that your brain can provide a new perspective and let your talents and skills shine.

Diversity is critical to the survival of any species. The challenge society faces is that someone decides what 'normal' is somewhere along the line and creates environments to support people who meet these expectations.

The problem comes for those of us with neurodivergent minds, when these environments don't support us, we are given labels of 'disorders' and offered drugs and tools to try and make us more 'normal'. We need a society that understands neurodiversity and creates inclusive environments for all of us.

Be proud of all you are.

ENVIRONMENT AND CONTEXT MATTER

You wouldn't judge a cat by its ability to swim or a fish by its ability to climb a tree, would you?

The same goes for your skills and abilities. What would it mean for you to be the fish swimming effortlessly in the clear waters or the cat climbing trees and sleeping in the sun?

This is why you need to understand your strengths and skills profoundly and use them for maximum impact to create the life you want to lead. Doing this will lead to an authentic life that combines balance, happiness, fulfilment and achievement.

If you deny your true strengths and force yourself to remain in challenging environments, where you force yourself to live in ways imposed on you by others, you have a recipe for a life of overwhelm, unhappiness and burnout. If you choose this life, you will constantly be trying to be someone you are not and will feel misunderstood, misaligned and unfulfilled.

Which life will you choose?

THE CATALYST FOR CHANGE

When I reflected on my life post-diagnosis, I saw myself and my experiences through a different lens. I spent over four decades in a state of high alert, desperate to figure out what I was 'allowed' to do. I'd become focused on the outward validation about whether I was good enough, acceptable and enough. The consensus felt like a firm 'no.'

In personal and social situations, things people liked about me when we met became what they disliked in the end, often my honesty and directness. Relationships and friendships fell away quickly, with rejection hitting hard. I was too sensitive, too outspoken, too blunt, too unpredictable, too rigid, too much, not enough. I felt faulty to my core.

At work, I was suffocated, silenced, ridiculed and scolded. My ideas didn't fit the organisation, the way I did things was too off-the-wall and my perfectionism never delivered the desired results. Each day, I felt like I stepped onto a stage, acted out a role and went home exhausted. It ended badly. At thirty-six, I exited corporate life forever and spent a year in a state of burnout, barely able to function.

Fast forward to now. I have over a decade of experience as an entrepreneur and can view these experiences through my new, post-diagnosis lens. I'm proud of myself for having endured all I did, and here's the funny thing: behaviours I processed as failings and weaknesses are some of my core strengths. I was in the wrong environment, with people who valued sameness, not uniqueness. I didn't have the confidence to be bold and stand by my ideas, opinions and beliefs. Instead, I'd tried to be compliant and it damn near killed me. Literally. I considered driving my car off the road one night on the drive home from my corporate job, desperate to escape it all. That was the catalyst for my resignation.

My key strength as an entrepreneur is my ability to see things differently and develop creative solutions. I'm not afraid to take risks and can make quick decisions, which is a gift. My honesty, directness and unapologetic existence have seen me win awards and be nominated for many more. My sensitivity means I can deeply connect with my clients. As a leader and manager, I create safe and supportive environments where I value everyone for who they are.

My hyperfocus and busy brain are my greatest gifts when I harness them correctly. I don't just 'know' things; I deeply know about things I'm passionate about. When I embrace how my brain works, I can achieve in one afternoon what many neurotypicals will take days or weeks to complete, if at all. I'm like a fast-track train with one destination in mind in those moments. And when the energy slump hits (and it will), I lean into it rather than try to push myself to keep going. I ignore the inner voice of my schoolteachers about my lack of focus; "She can do it when she puts her mind to it, but she can be lazy and easily distracted." It turns out I'm neither; I have this crazy, beautiful brain that is supercharged with magic and often feels it's wired up to the National Grid and has *all* the energy supply! I love it.

My metaphor for my life is a garden full of wildflowers, with a sunflower in the centre. The sunflower continues to grow, reaches for the sun, and is in the garden's centre. It represents my personal growth, evolution and desire to reach for a life that feels warm and inviting. The wildflowers represent the unpredictable world that we live in and remind us to expect the unexpected and see new opportunities and experiences. The wildflowers also represent my purpose and vision for the future: to make an impact and catalyse change for our neurodivergent community, ensuring younger generations have more positive experiences. Seeds from wildflowers are picked up in the wind and transported far and wide. We never know how far they will reach or where they will land, but new areas of beautiful wildflowers will emerge when they do. And the cycle will continue whilst I continue to tend to the sunflower.

Perhaps you can think of your own metaphor for your ideal life, something powerful and meaningful that you can connect to when you want to remind yourself of why you're here, working through these pages.

SUMMARY

Deeply understanding and accepting yourself and all your attributes can transform your life. You'll find freedom when you move to a place of self-acceptance and release the need to fit into the vanilla idea of what others want and expect from you.

Understand that your neurodivergent mind brings great strengths and skills that are unique to you. Use them to increase your confidence and sense of fulfilment. Become clear on your strengths and reframe any negative feedback (real or perceived), which will help you focus on the value you add.

Let go of the belief that you are somehow less or not good enough and remember that you are extraordinary. You are different, not less.

In the next chapter, we move on to 'Discover,' where we look at your core values, passions and goals for the future. Get excited for this one; it's magical.

TOP FIVE TAKE-AWAYS

1. Accept and embrace yourself exactly as you are.
2. You cannot make your beautiful, neurodivergent mind work like a neurotypical mind, so don't try to.
3. Stop trying to fit in and start proudly standing out.
4. Understand and harness your strengths to create a life where you feel fulfilled, happy and successful.
5. You inspire others by being your true and authentic self. Your actions show others what is possible for them.

4

—————

DISCOVER

The Discover stage guides you to create a life aligned with your values. You'll discover what matters most to you and why, and you will understand how living that life looks and feels for you.

Focusing on your core values is the critical component of RADIATE. You will be able to use them as an internal compass for all your decisions. Don't worry if you're not clear on your core values yet; you will be by the end of this chapter.

An important point on values, you may believe you have strong values, but as you work through this pillar of RADIATE, you may realise that you are not aligned with them. If you had asked me to share my values before going through RADIATE, I would have told you exactly what they were. But, when I looked at my life, I realised I was too busy living on other people's terms and most of my values fell by the wayside. I continually felt uneasy, unfulfilled and disconnected from myself because I wasn't aligned with my values.

The problem was that when I chose my old values, I picked words that mattered, but I had never considered how to live by them. I also chose familiar words that I thought others would approve of and required little explanation.

When I chose my new set of values, I ensured they were ones which I really connected with and I was clear on what living by these values looked and felt like for me. I took time to consider them and why they were important to me and I imagined multiple ways to live by them. My old values, such as authenticity, integrity and honesty, have now naturally become a part of me as I live as my true self.

When you have clear values you are connected to, you can adapt your life to align with them. You will be able to identify ways to align your life and use them as your internal compass to guide you. Over time, this will become subconscious, natural and automatic.

Living a life aligned with your values will make you feel calmer, happier and more balanced. Your values are the secret to a life that is fulfilled, happy and successful.

VALUES, PASSIONS AND PURPOSE

To live a life where balance, inner peace and fulfilment exist simultaneously, you must bring together your values, passions and vision for the future (or life goals, if you prefer that term).

Values

First, let's look at values. This is a *crucial* step in the RADIATE model; please do not rush this. It is essential that you choose values that you connect to and can live by. It is vital that you choose the right values for you, otherwise, the whole RADIATE model becomes ineffective. Do not choose values according to what other people think you should have or ones you believe you 'should' have; choose values that have real meaning for you.

When you let your values guide your choices, decisions and actions, you *can* transform your entire life into one that brings a strong sense of calm, happiness, success and connection.

Your values may change throughout your life as your responsibilities or circumstances evolve, such as starting a family or a new business venture, however, some of your core values, which guide how you treat others, will likely remain the same.

You will discover and become clear on your values further in this chapter, so hold tight for now.

Passions and Purpose

In this context, passions are the things you love to do that light you up, motivate you and get you excited. Your passion(s) can be simple; there are no defining criteria.

Purpose is your deeper reason for doing what you do, what you truly care about. A great way to home in on your current purpose(s) is to use Dean Graziosi's Seven Layers Deep exercise[8]

---

8. https://www.deangraziosi.com/wp–content/uploads/2021/03/7–Levels–Deep–Exercise.pdf

Initial Desire/Goal: I want to grow my business.

- **Why #1:** Because I want it to be more profitable.
- **Why #2:** So that I can earn more money.
- **Why #3:** Because I want to provide better for my family.
- **Why #4:** So that they can have more opportunities.
- **Why #5:** Because I want them to be happy and fulfilled.
- **Why #6:** So that they can live a meaningful life.
- **Why #7:** Because seeing my family thrive and knowing I contributed to it gives me a deep sense of purpose.

Your purpose doesn't have to be work-related. You could use this exercise for a personal goal.

Initial Desire/Goal: I want to learn a new hobby.

- **Why #1:** Because I want to do something fun in my spare time.
- **Why #2:** Because I want to learn a new skill and be creative.
- **Why #3:** Because it helps me take my mind off work.
- **Why #4:** So that I can relax, de-stress and avoid burnout.
- **Why #5:** Because mastering something new makes me feel good about myself and increases my confidence.
- **Why #6:** So that I can enjoy my personal time more and create balance in my life.
- **Why #7:** Because feeling happy and fulfilled in my personal time improves my overall life satisfaction and experiences.

The words 'passion' and 'purpose' can feel loaded when someone tells us to find them. It's singular and sounds like we must pick one thing and stick to it for the rest of our lives.

Your passions and purpose will likely change throughout your life; you do not need to pick one thing now and commit to it forever. The RADIATE model will always meet you where you're at, so it doesn't matter if your passions or purpose change along the way. Remember that they align with your vision and goals, as they influence how you live your life.

What are your passions and purpose?

Spend some time reflecting on these. There is a link to the Seven Layers Deep worksheet and an example at the back of this book.

LIVING LIFE ON YOUR TERMS

Does living life on your terms sound a bit far-fetched or damn near impossible right now? If you have spent decades being a prolific people-pleaser to keep everyone else happy, this might feel as realistic as time travel. But you can do this.

It will be uncomfortable at times, but it will be worth it in the long run; those small moments of discomfort will pale into insignificance.

With healthy boundaries in place, which we will come to later in the book, you will have the tools and confidence to create a happy and fulfilling life on your terms, unapologetically.

When you change your life to live on your terms, you might experience resistance from others. That's perfectly normal and we will cover how to manage this when we reach Advocate in the RADIATE model.

This is a gentle nudge of reassurance to let you know that you *can* create the life you want and I will show you how.

COGNITIVE DISSONANCE

Have you ever felt a nagging unease when you do something that doesn't fit your natural way of thinking or being?

Think about it, maybe you're at a social event that's loud and overwhelming and all you want is to step outside and breathe, but instead, you force yourself to stay and mingle because that seems socially acceptable.

Maybe honesty is one of your core values but you find yourself in a group of people and exaggerate your recent successes to fit in with the group who are sharing their big wins. This small act feels uncomfortable because it clashes with your fundamental belief in authenticity and truthfulness.

In each case, you're acting against your instincts to please others or to adhere to what you believe is societally expected or acceptable.

That uneasy sensation is called cognitive dissonance. It's like having two opposing thoughts in your head at the same time or acting in a way that contradicts your personal values, and it can feel uncomfortable and awkward.

For many neurodivergent women, the challenge of aligning personal actions with inner beliefs and values can be particularly striking when it comes to people-pleasing. If you've ever found yourself saying yes when every fibre in your being wanted to say no, you've experienced cognitive dissonance.

This discomfort isn't just annoying; it's a signal from your subconscious that something isn't right. It's pushing you to resolve the contradiction, to bring your actions back in line with your beliefs. Why? Living in harmony with our values is key to feeling balance, happiness and peace.

If you ignore the dissonance, it can lead to stress, anxiety, and a feeling of disconnection from yourself and others, as you're not behaving as your true self. When you act in a way that matches your beliefs and values, life feels right, and you will naturally be happier and more confident.

When you feel that itch of cognitive dissonance, listen to it and see it as an opportunity to pause, reflect and realign. It's like recalibrating your internal compass to ensure it is pointing towards your true north – towards a life that genuinely reflects who you are.

Understanding cognitive dissonance is particularly potent for neurodivergent women, who might feel pressured to mask their natural tendencies in order to blend into social or professional settings. Here's the thing: every time you put on a mask to please others, ignoring your true self, you send yourself a message that other people's comfort is more important than yours. It is not.

Notice when you feel the unease or inner conflict. Pay attention to what is happening for you in these moments and use these experiences to help realign and create a life that *does* feel good for you.

CONNECT WITH YOUR CORE VALUES

We've covered a lot of ground so far. You have reflected on your life and created a vision for the future, which includes your passions, purpose and goals. Before you go any further, I'd like to choose your top five core values. This is essential before you move on. RADIATE will not work effectively for you if you don't invest the time to do this.

When you choose your values, consider *why* they are important and think of examples of what each value would look and feel like when you live by it. This is important because it is easy to choose a word that you think is a good value to have, but if you can't identify why it matters to you or what it would mean to live by that value, then it's not one of your core values.

We can subconsciously choose values we think we should have – values passed down from our family, or values imposed by society or culture. Connecting your why and identifying examples of what living with that value at the heart of your life is like for you will ensure it's one you can live by daily. You use the Sever Layers Deep exercise here to help you deeply connect with a value.

Here are a couple of examples to help get you started.

Choosing authenticity as a value could mean being true to yourself in your thoughts, words and actions. You could live by this value by consistently making sure that your decisions and behaviours reflect your genuine beliefs and feelings.

Choosing balance as a core value could mean ensuring your work, personal life and relationships each get the attention they deserve so that you feel fulfilled in each area of your life. You could live by this value by regularly assessing how you spend your time and energy and giving yourself permission to pause, reflect and align your choices with your well-being to ensure that no area of your life overwhelms the other or yourself.

If you struggle to come up with values, the Resources section at the back of this book has a list to give you some ideas. However, many additional values exist, so please don't limit yourself to those. A quick search on Google will also bring up many examples.

Doing this exercise before you go any further into these pages is vital. Do not skip this or rush ahead.

HOW DOES IT LOOK AND FEEL, LIVING IN AND OUT OF ALIGNMENT?

Most values exercises stop there once you have created your list. But it is not enough to just create a list. They must have true meaning and you must be able to envisage living with those values daily.

The next step is to reflect on situations or circumstances where you feel you have lived in alignment with your values and where you haven't. Make two separate lists – one list of times when you *were* in alignment and another for when you were *not*. Split the list into different life areas, such as work, personal and social.

These could be specific times in your life, or they might be as simple as an action or experience you had. When you focus on these areas, you become familiar with what being in and out of alignment with your values means for you and what that looks and feels like. This isn't a fault-finding exercise. Be radically honest with yourself through a lens of self-compassion and acceptance. You are gathering valuable insights and information to enable you to live in alignment with your values in the future.

Identify as much detail as you can.

- What were you doing?
- Who was there?
- What was the environment or circumstances?
- How were you feeling at the time? (For example, were you tired, emotional, overwhelmed, happy, exhilarated or calm).
- How did you feel when you acted in or out of alignment with your values?
- Did you have any physical signs or symptoms?

This exercise identifies any themes or patterns, such as specific circumstances, certain people or situations that influence your ability to make decisions in line with your values.

Think about whether you experience any physical symptoms. What were they? Where did you feel them? Was it pain, discomfort or a different sensation?

Examples of physical symptoms of not being aligned with your values are:

- Nausea, dizziness, stomach ache, headaches, anxiety, panic, inability to think straight, sweating, shallow breathing.

Examples of physical symptoms when you *are* aligned with your values are:

- Relaxed muscles, clarity of thought, butterflies of excitement, calm breathing.

If you have identified values that are new to you and that you would like to live your life by, reflect on hypothetical situations where you can imagine what living in alignment with these values will mean for you. Then go on to also identify what living out of alignment would be like for you. This will give you a comparison and insights into how you will know when you are in or out of alignment with your values.

YOUR INTERNAL COMPASS

The exercises you have just completed allow you to fully connect with your values on multiple levels. This is how they become your internal compass. When you are clear about your values and connected to them, you can intuitively use them to guide your choices and decisions.

If living in alignment with your values is new to you, then it may feel alien at first, but it will get easier with time. The more you do it, the easier it becomes until it becomes a subconscious process.

Using your values alongside the vision you created for your life is a powerful tool to ensure you make aligned choices that help you build and live your desired life.

BRINGING YOUR VALUES INTO YOUR LIFE

Taking steps to align with your values doesn't need to involve big actions. The thought of significant change can halt you if it feels too big or unachievable. Instead, focus on how you can bring your values into daily activities with small changes and new micro habits.

For example, if one of your values is compassion, start with some self-compassion at a time when you might have expressed negative self-talk.

If connection is your value, smile at a stranger or compliment someone. Small actions like asking a work colleague how they are or buying them a coffee are a great start.

If creativity is a value, could you find an opportunity to do something creative? This could be a creative activity or a thought process, whichever works best for you.

If courage is a value, could you take a small step out of your comfort zone and send a message to someone you'd like to collaborate with, work with, or compliment them on a recent achievement?

Go big and bold if you'd like! But often, the small actions have the most impact and will help you build your confidence and recognise where you can bring your values into your life daily.

When making bigger decisions in my life, I find that when I ask myself the simple question, "Does this align with my values (and vision)?" I gain so much clarity. Try it. Sit with the question for as long as you need to and see what comes up. With time and practice, you will start to tap into the internal compass of your values that will help to guide you.

IS YOUR LIFE VISION ALIGNED WITH YOUR VALUES?

Revisit your vision board or life story vision (or whichever format you chose to capture your vision) and make sure you have aligned your values, passions and purpose with your vision for the future. Considering your values, reflect on whether the vision you created aligns or whether you had made choices based on what you believed you 'should' be doing, not what you *want* to do. Make any adjustments you need to make with your values as your internal compass to guide you.

Revisit your vision board or life vision every three to six months to ensure that your visions, goals, passions and values remain aligned.

 *NEWSFLASH*
Your values, passions, purpose, and visions
are not fixed.

They are fluid and you are free to change them. Use them to enhance and guide your life, not restrict it or tie you down.

When you have a neurodivergent brain, reviewing your choices regularly is essential and helpful to avoid getting stuck on a path that takes you away from the life you desire.

TRUE VALUES

The first time I worked on my values was after I experienced a spectacular year-long burnout at thirty-six. After over a decade of enduring the struggles, I left my legal management career forever. I was lost; my whole identity had been wrapped up in my legal career and without that, I didn't know who I was anymore. Shame washed over me. This was more evidence that I couldn't cope in the adult world. Others told me so, telling me I was an idiot for leaving and I should 'pull myself together' and go back. They thought I 'had it all'. I didn't dare tell them that I had considered driving off the road one night, as I came home from work, just so I didn't have to do it anymore.

A few months into my recovery, I listened to The Firestarter Sessions, by Danielle La Porte,[9] and Big Magic, by Elizabeth Gilbert,[10] on Audible. I wanted to find my values, passions and that elusive word, 'purpose'. I felt worthless and I was desperate to feel worthy.

I picked out values that connected with me. They were *authenticity, honesty, integrity, compassion and determination.* If you'd asked me at any point, post-2012, what my values were, I'd have reeled those out to you and firmly believed I lived by them.

It wasn't until my autism and ADHD diagnosis, when I revisited my values, that I realised I was not in alignment with them at all, except determination. Here's what I discovered when I revisited the values I'd aligned to in 2012.

Authenticity: I spent my whole life trying to fit in and be accepted, not being my authentic self. I lived in a state of constant cognitive dissonance – value fail.

Honesty: I was honest with my opinions and what I said to others, but I wasn't honest about how I felt or what I wanted. Not with others and not with myself – value fail.

Integrity: Yes and no. In my interaction with others, I acted with integrity, but this was more in line with the outward persona I had created to blend in and survive. I have very strong moral principles, but sometimes, these become a

---

9. https://www.audible.co.uk/pd/The–Fire–Starter–Sessions–Audiobook/B007SY96II

10. https://www.audible.co.uk/pd/Big–Magic–Audiobook/B012YGQ5PG

barrier to interactions, as I cannot articulate them as my true self.

Compassion: For others, yes; for myself, *no*. My self-compassion was non-existent; I was my worst critic and used to beat myself up daily with a barrage of how useless I was and how I needed to try harder and do better.

Reflecting on my life, I was astounded and ashamed that I was completely misaligned to my values. I went back to the start, revisited the values exercises I had done over a decade ago and decided to look at it differently.

I wanted to discover how to align my life with my core values and use them as my internal compass. This set me free, no joke. Now, I believe I automatically act with authenticity, integrity and honesty in every part of my life. Here are my newly aligned values.

Curiosity: to have an approach of loving curiosity, to keep my mind open to new experiences so I can learn and grow. To be curious and accept others without judgement.

Courage: To do the things I'm afraid of. Fear is just excitement that needs an attitude adjustment! Courage opens me up to new experiences, which satisfies my ADHD need for newness and adventure! If I choose courage, I can also find ways to balance my autistic need for routine and sameness.

Connection: To show up authentically to create genuine and meaningful connections with others who align with my values.

Compassion: For myself and others, to listen to individual experiences and to believe the experiences of others, even if (especially if) they don't match my own.

Empowerment: To inspire and empower others to take bold actions for their own lives and create a better and more inclusive future for future generations.

These values are my internal compass, and they are behind every decision I make. At first, it was a conscious process where I asked myself, "Does this action or decision align with my values?" and I'd wait for the feedback from my brain and body. Today, it is second nature to me. I can recognise how it feels in my body when I am in or out of alignment, and I use that as my guide. When I am unsure or overwhelmed, I give myself time and space before I decide. I will always choose alignment, even if it's the harder choice or may be met with resistance from others. I know the consequences of not being aligned; I had decades of experience and it's not a place I will return to.

SUMMARY

In this chapter, you've learned the importance of aligning with your core values. Your values are your internal compass and if you tune into them, they will be a powerful guide to help you create a happy life where you feel fulfilled – a life where you get to define success on *your* terms.

When you live by your values, you will be empowered to release the pressure to live up to other people's or societal expectations. You'll feel calmer and happier because you will make choices that feel good for you.

You'll discover that the anxiety and pressure that you've experienced when you try and force yourself to conform to what others expect of you will lift.

You might think this all sounds good but have no idea how to make these changes or shifts in your life. Don't worry; that's where we're heading next!

TOP FIVE TAKE-AWAYS

1. Your values are your internal compass. Let them guide you.
2. Consider your values alongside your vision for the future to guide you to create your desired life.
3. It's OK if identifying your values initially feels challenging. Don't rush; you can revisit them as needed.
4. Understand what living in and out of alignment looks and feels like. This will enable you to make intuitive decisions.
5. Find ways to bring your values into your life daily. This will help you see the big and small opportunities that align with your life.

5

INNOVATE

In this chapter, you will discover what support you need in areas you find difficult to navigate.

I chose 'Innovate' for the 'I' in RADIATE because I want you to think beyond the traditional strategies and tools you have seen or tried before and weigh up what you need in different situations and environments based on your unique experiences. Move beyond what you believe you are 'allowed'; get creative and find solutions that work for you.

In the first six months following my diagnosis, I tried many tools and techniques recommended to me. I didn't think about what I needed; I accepted what was offered, which, in most cases, made my life harder. I realised something very important then, and you need to understand this before you go any further…

Most of the tools, advice, and techniques available to us are designed to make our brains work in a neurotypical way, to be more 'normal'. They set you up for failure because you cannot change how your wonderful brain works. Society needs to consider how to adapt to *us* to create more inclusivity, not for us to force our brains to act in a way that they can't.

When you reflect on what *you* need and want, think beyond what you already know is available. Give thought to what will enable you to thrive and live a successful and happy life on *your* terms.

You can develop solutions and strategies that feel a little bonkers; that's great. Just because you haven't seen anyone else do it doesn't mean you can't. What matters is that you structure your life in a way that allows you to manage areas that you need support with.

THERE ARE NO PRIZES FOR DOING LIFE IN HARD MODE!

Does life seem much more challenging than it should be? Do you look at others and wonder why they can cope better or easily do things you struggle with or can't do?

Life is not easy. Life will always bring challenges, struggles, and difficult experiences. I'm not sure where it happened, but society seemed to buy into a belief somewhere along the line that life was supposed to be easy. Maybe it was the fairy tales we were told as children. Perhaps it's the smoke screen of social media, where we are constantly shown images and tales of people living their best lives – seemingly with ease.

Life isn't easy and releasing that belief might take some pressure off.

When I talk about doing life in 'hard mode', I'm talking about the *additional* effort and challenges that we, as neurodivergent women deal with on top of the usual life struggles that neurotypicals experience.

This is why it is essential for you to deeply understand your challenges and areas you find difficult and create a supportive environment for yourself. Life is hard enough as it is without forcing yourself to live in 'hard mode' by ignoring your needs and wants to keep others happy.

LIVING LIFE ON OTHER PEOPLE'S TERMS

We know we are masters at living on everyone else's terms. We put others' needs before our own, even if the consequences to our well-being or enjoyment of life are negatively impacted.

Living on other people's terms is a one-way road to overwhelm, exhaustion and unhappiness. It can lead to anxiety and mental health struggles. Resentment can build and cause damage to your relationships and connections with others (and yourself). The cumulative result will leave you miserable, isolated and burnt out.

That is why you will start to live life on *your* terms now. You can take control of your life and make decisions that enable you to lead a happy, balanced and fulfilling life, without apology.

Of course, this doesn't mean stampeding through life, demanding everyone does things your way. It's about finding ways to improve your experiences and connections without constant compromise and sacrifice on your part.

A little word of caution here. You may have people in your life who are used to you doing things on their terms and the thought of doing things on your terms seems scary, impossible or too difficult to face. Don't worry. The changes you need to make are easier than you might expect.

WHAT YOU NEED VERSUS WHAT YOU PERCEIVE YOU'RE ALLOWED

Over a decade ago, a talking therapist presented me with the scenario below. I didn't appreciate this exercise at the time, but it came back to me after my diagnosis. Think about your answers as we go through this scenario and questions:

Scenario

You're at a party and someone hands you a tray of cupcakes. There are vanilla cupcakes with blue icing and chocolate cupcakes with pink icing.

Q: What do you do with the tray?

I responded that I would pass the tray around the room without taking one.

Q: What if the tray returns to you and none are left?

My response was that it would be OK, except I didn't mean it – I would have been disappointed I didn't have a cupcake.

Q: What if the tray returns to you with only a vanilla and blue icing cupcake left, but you want a chocolate one with pink icing?

I told her again that I would be OK with that, but honestly, I would have been disappointed.

She used this simple exercise to highlight that I put everyone else's needs and wants before mine. Maybe you answered the same as me, or perhaps you made sure you had a cupcake?

If you took a cupcake, then that's amazing but, the exercise isn't over yet…

She then asked this question, which feels relevant to this chapter.

> Q: What if you wanted the chocolate cupcake with *blue* icing, not pink?

I told her I couldn't have that. When she asked me why, I told her it wasn't an option; it wasn't available. It wasn't allowed.

From there, our conversation focused on how I made decisions and choices based on what I believed was allowed or permitted for me. I never dared to ask for something different or communicate what I wanted or needed.

Here's what I want you to take from this cake analogy.

- Take a cake from the damn tray before you pass it around. Put your needs and wants first.
- Choose the cake you want; don't wait to see what – if anything – is left.
- If the cake you want isn't available, ask for what you do want. Don't assume something isn't possible just because you can't see it, or it's not been offered to you.

It's an insightful exercise that demonstrates the importance of putting your wants and needs first, rather than everyone else's.

The difference between a need and a want, in this context, are:

A need is essential to live and function. A want improves your quality of life.

The lines can be blurred as we interchange the two in modern society. Think about a need as something you require to live in a way that makes you feel safe and supported. Consider a want as something that you desire and would enhance your experiences or life but is not essential to your existence.

Both are important to create your optimum life. Wants are not selfish, despite what you might have been told in the past. In childhood, I was told, "I want doesn't get." If this sounds familiar, drop that belief right here.

You are not selfish. If you look around, you'll find evidence of other people taking what they want and need unapologetically. What do you think if you see others behaving this way? Do you wish you could put your wants and needs first, or do you see these people as selfish, greedy, demanding or pushy, and you don't want to be like that?

Putting your needs and wants first isn't selfish, and you do not need to act in an undesirable way to do this. Having your needs met is about self-respect, self-care, and an understanding that your well-being is the foundation from which you do everything. When you take care of yourself, you are better equipped to contribute positively and fully to those around you in all areas of your life.

You are not asking for the ridiculous or impossible, you simply want to create a life with balance, where you are not unnecessarily doing life in hard mode.

MAXIMISE YOUR STRENGTHS

Earlier you read about how magic occurs when you focus on your strengths; consider this a reminder.

Research has shown that having a strength-based approach to life is the key to success and happiness.[11] It's also been proven to reduce anxiety and depression and promote feelings of positivity.[12]

When you harness and appreciate your strengths, the impact goes beyond contributing to your success alone. It has a positive impact on your well-being and confidence.

Every individual will have challenges, including neurotypicals. The difference is that society is not set up to understand or accommodate those of us who are neurodivergent; it's created for neurotypicals. This increases the challenges we experience and leaves us unsupported.

You do not need to apologise for your challenges or feel that you are in some way less. This is a societal problem; we must confidently advocate for ourselves unapologetically, with the knowledge that, over time, society will adapt.

The difficulties you experience come as a direct result of society not understanding or accommodating the rich diversity within the human species. You are not broken, less capable or in any way less, your brain simply processes life in a different way – a pretty cool way, in my opinion!

---

11. https://workwithimpact.co.uk/news/benefits–of–a–strength–based–approach/

12. https://www.ncbi.nlm.nih.gov/pmc/articles/PMC3939995/

FINDING YOUR CREATIVE SOLUTIONS AND SUPPORT

It's time to create innovative ways to structure your life to work for you to ensure you feel calm and supported and can live life on your terms. Remember the power of ADE model we covered in Chapter Three. This is the perfect place to start. Don't waste time finding ways to support yourself in tasks you don't need to do.

- Automate: Which areas of your life can you automate?
- Delegate: Who else can do a task or offer support?
- Eliminate: Remove anything unnecessary.

Now that you've done that, brainstorm how you'd like your life to be structured. What do you need to maximise your strengths, follow your passions and feel supported and safe in challenging areas? You may find it easier to break your life into different sections, such as professional, home/personal and social life.

Think about these things:

- What do you need to feel safe, supported and calm?
- What do you want that will enhance your life experiences?
- Who do you need around you to feel connected and loved?

Get your ideas out of your head and write them down. Please don't stop and think whether you believe them to be possible.

The two exercises below can be helpful; one is for the present moment, and one is for the future. If you don't like visualising exercises, then simply think about the scenarios and write your thoughts down or record voice notes.

Present Moment:

Sit with your eyes closed. Imagine your ideal day in your ideal life. See it in as much detail as possible, from when you get up to when you go to bed. Imagine, in vivid colour, what you are doing, what you can see, hear, smell and touch. Connect with how you feel; notice who you interact with and your daily activities. Notice how your interactions and day flow. Write down as many details as you can. Then, read through your ideal day and identify what you would need to be able to live it. Note your thoughts on how you could enhance your life to have the desired experiences.

I allow ten to fifteen minutes for this exercise, but you can make this shorter or longer.

Future:

Imagine a conversation with your future self, five years from now. Imagine going for a walk or coffee with them and asking how they are. Ask what they've been doing and how they have achieved this amazing life. Ask them to tell you how they got there and how they feel about everything. I found this a beautiful exercise for imagining and living my future life. Conversing with my future self was also insightful, and I got answers I didn't expect. Being able to detach from reality and imagine myself as a different person helped me achieve a different perspective.

Alternatively, you might like to do a future-self meditation exercise, which you will find in the References section of this book.

DON'T BE AFRAID TO ASK

You may feel scared to ask for adjustments, considerations or support.

 ## *NEWSFLASH*

Please remember that you are not asking for the world; you just want to create a safe and calm life where you can thrive and be happy and successful.

You deserve to live on your terms. And here's another beautiful thought: by advocating for yourself, you are part of a movement to shift society's perception of what autism and ADHD are – different, not less. Maybe you know you're neurodivergent or suspect you might be. Perhaps you've always felt a bit different or quirky and others have called you odd or weird. By showing up as your true, authentic self, you are showing others that we do not all need to conform to societal standards of 'normal' and that there is incredible value, richness and beauty in embracing neurodiversity.

Every time we share our experiences and advocate for ourselves, we increase our understanding of our needs, increasing the likelihood that society will adapt to accommodate all of us rather than expecting us to suffer and struggle while trying to live in a society not designed for us.

Don't put the book down now out of fear. We move on to how to advocate for yourself in the next chapter, so hold tight for now.

HERE ARE SOME SUGGESTIONS AND IDEAS

You will find your unique way to create a balanced and supported life, but here are some ideas to get you started.

Work Environment:

- Think about the noise levels, lighting and working environment. Do you struggle with any element of these?

- What do you need to work at your optimum? Perhaps a quiet space, dimmer lighting or to work from home on certain days of the week. Could you invest in ear Loops, earphones or apps for focus and planning? Would a standing desk help, or an inflatable core stability ball, instead of a chair?

- How is your day structured? Are there lots of interruptions, distractions, or a lack of structure? Would it help to schedule meetings for specific days, have set times when your team can access you, or could you delegate some activities to others? Do you work better at certain times of the day, such as early morning?

This is an important note if you have a job that makes it difficult to make workplace adjustments, such as teaching and nursing, for example. You may be able to introduce tools such as ear loops to help with noise, apps for meditation/ breath work, or perhaps take your lunch break somewhere quieter, but bigger accommodations may not be possible.

When work accommodations are difficult, focus on what you would benefit from after work or in other areas of your life to minimise overwhelm and create balance.

Personal Life

- Is your home a calm and safe space for you? What do you need to feel comfortable at home? Perhaps get help from family around the house, hire a cleaner, or create a sensory space for you where you can go to destress and relax.

- Do you have time to do things you enjoy? Could you create a space in your house to do the things you love and allocate time to them each week? Whether it's reading, exercise, or creative pursuits, set yourself up in a space that makes it easy to do activities that bring you joy.

- Does being outside in nature calm you? Can you find ways to spend more time outside, perhaps incorporating work meetings into walks?

Social Life

- Do your friends make you feel good and do you enjoy spending time with them? Prioritise your time for people who make you feel good and step away from those who don't. Create boundaries that protect your energy.

- Do you enjoy activities with friends or do you force yourself to go to places that overwhelm you? Could you suggest different activities or locations to meet?

- Or do you love the activities you do, but need to plan a day to recover after social interactions?

THE RIGHT TOOLS

The months that followed my diagnosis were some of the most difficult times in my life. I had initially felt relief that now I knew why my life had been the way it was.

I enthusiastically threw myself into working with coaches. I embraced the tools and techniques and believed that life would get better. Except it didn't. It got worse.

Several months in, I realised that the tools and techniques I was desperately trying to use were designed to make my brain behave in a neurotypical way – a recipe for disaster.

Being autistic and ADHD, I had been able to hyperfocus on newfound tools or techniques and made them a part of my routine. The ADHD excitement of something new, coupled with my autistic need for routine, made it possible for me to maintain these new ways of working for a short while, but the effort and energy they required to force my brain to work unnaturally meant nothing lasted longer than a couple of weeks.

When nothing worked, my anxiety increased and I eventually gave up. It triggered familiar feelings of shame and I felt like a failure. I was beyond help. However, when I stopped trying to force my brain to act in an unnatural way, my mindset shifted and I got curious about my unique brain.

I had to find a way to balance a brain that often opposes itself. The ADHD part of me can be impulsive and excitable and needs newness, whilst the autistic part of me hates change and the unknown and loves routine. I saw a great meme that had the perfect description for my ADHD brain:

"It helps if you imagine ADHD as a tiny little elf in your head who's trying so hard to be helpful but is in fact quite drunk."

On the other hand, my autistic brain is like an overprotective parent and a strict headmistress rolled into one. It likes to know precisely what will happen, in which order and who will be present. It needs to know plans A, B, C and D, and it needs a clear escape route to safety when things don't go to plan.

Finding harmony between these two very different parts of my brain is difficult at the best of times. Throw stress and anxiety into the mix, and it's like watching a tightrope artist at the circus without a safety net to catch them!

Here are three things I've introduced that have enhanced my experiences.

Time and Task Management

I ditched the time planners and apps. I accepted that my brain was never going to work in the same way as a neurotypical. Instead, I learned how my energy levels and brain work. I now have tasks I want to achieve by the end of each week and month, but I allow myself to select from the list depending on my energy levels that day. I can pick tasks that need my undivided attention on my hyperfocus days. I'll pick easier and quicker tasks when my energy and focus are lower. Everything moves me in the right direction whilst allowing for freedom and adjustments.

I also permit myself to step away from it all if I feel overwhelmed and heading for burnout.

Take time to understand your early warning signs so you can step away and recover. Please don't push yourself to keep going when you need to rest; the consequences are not worth it.

Sensory Overload

My ear loops are my best friend. I use the Loops Switch ear loops, at the time of writing. I can switch between total sound block to ambient or conversational. Reducing sensory overload has been so good for my anxiety.

At home, I have created a sensory haven on my sofa: weighted blankets, soft, fluffy throws, and big pillows. I can collapse into the softness and bury myself in blankets, which helps to calm my senses and nervous system.

I also have a 'worry' ring that spins, which I can instantly access if overload hits me unexpectedly when I am out.

Asking for Support Without Apology

I used to believe asking for help or support was a sign of weakness, proof that I couldn't cope. My diagnosis changed that. I realised I didn't need to struggle the way I had been. I found that when I asked for support, life became easier.

If I am going to events, I'll ask to sit on the outside of a room, so I am not surrounded by noise. If I attend meetings, I request a quiet location to avoid distractions. And I have to go to hospital, I explain I am autistic and have ADHD and how that affects me due to anxiety of the unknown. I request that no junior members of staff treat me, no students in my room and I explain that I might panic because it takes me time to recognise what is happening in my body when I am unwell or injured. I ask for patience, kindness and clarity.

If I need to share that I am autistic or have ADHD, I always remember that I am sharing it to make my experiences more comfortable. I never apologise for asking for help or accommodation. I no longer apologise for who I am.

SUMMARY

Congratulations. You now know what you want and need to enable you to live on your terms. You are a giant step closer to a happy, fulfilled and successful life.

Approach your desires with loving curiosity. Find ways to innovate and develop ideas that support you. Remember, you can set your life up in any way you desire; you do not need the permission of others.

Never apologise for the support and accommodations you request; you do not need to apologise for how your wonderful brain works. The issue isn't your brain; the issue is that society is not set up to support your uniqueness, and that needs to change.

Speaking of advocacy, that's where we are heading now. Get ready to confidently communicate your needs and wants to the outside world!

TOP FIVE TAKE-AWAYS

1. Living on other people's terms quickly leads to burnout and feeling overwhelmed.
2. Focus on what you need and want, not what you believe you're allowed.
3. You can have the chocolate cupcake with the blue icing if you want it.
4. Consider ways to improve your experiences and connections with others in all areas of your life.
5. Don't forget to Automate, Delegate or Eliminate!

6

ADVOCATE

In this chapter, you will learn how to advocate for yourself confidently and unapologetically.

For the RADIATE model, advocate means to ask for what you want and need, without apology.

Healthy boundaries are vital when you advocate for yourself. We focus on them a lot in this chapter. You'll discover why healthy boundaries are essential to your well-being and success in all life areas, along with how to create, communicate and ensure others honour them.

If you have no idea what I mean by boundaries, don't worry, we will cover that now.

You'll learn helpful tricks and tips that you can use to relieve the pressure and anxiety if you find yourself in situations where you find it difficult to say 'no'.

It's time to take action, so, let's get stuck in.

ADVOCATING FROM A PLACE OF HEALTHY BOUNDARIES

If you have lived as a prolific people-pleaser, the chances are you've lived without boundaries.

Think of boundaries as the invisible lines you draw to protect your well-being and respect your needs and values.

They are guidelines that help you define how you want to be treated by others, what you are comfortable with and what's unacceptable. They can be physical, emotional or mental. These boundaries ensure that you are treated with respect and consideration.

It is important to understand that boundaries are something that you set for yourself, not to control the actions of other people, but to establish what you are willing and unwilling to accept.

And it's a two-way street; it also involves you being respectful of the boundaries of others in return.

Healthy boundaries aren't selfish; they are crucial for maintaining self-respect, personal integrity and mental and emotional health.

THE IMPORTANCE OF HEALTHY BOUNDARIES WHEN ADVOCATING FOR YOURSELF

Think of your boundaries as an invisible shield of protection. They should align with your values, wants and needs and enable you to live a safe, fulfilling and supported life.

Communicating your boundaries to others lets them know what is acceptable for you and what is not. They can also serve as an effective filter for people in your life, as you will attract and connect with others when you have mutual respect for boundaries.

Your boundaries will create a calm and happy life and stop people-pleasing tendencies in their tracks. Anxiety and over-whelm levels will reduce, while your sense of balance and happiness will soar.

THE CONSEQUENCES OF UNHEALTHY BOUNDARIES

It is impossible to advocate for yourself without healthy boundaries. In fact, when you have no boundaries in place to protect you, you are vulnerable. You will find others take advantage of you and expect you to do things on their terms. With unhealthy boundaries, you risk emotional burnout, overwhelm, loss of self-esteem, and entanglement in toxic relationships and friendships.

You risk taking on more than you can cope with in all areas of your life, and being overwhelmed in one area will have a knock-on effect in another, which is why it's essential to have boundaries in all areas of your life.

When you regularly allow others to overstep your limits, you can end up with chronic stress and mental fatigue, which will negatively impact not just your emotional well-being but also your physical health. There is a lot of research to support the physical impact of emotional stress on the body too.[13]

---

13. https://www.newscientist.com/article/mg25634132–300–why–emotions–can–feel–so–painful–and–what–it–means–for–painkillers/

NEWSFLASH

Healthy boundaries are your protectors.
They are necessary for your very existence.

FEAR OF JUDGEMENT AND REJECTION

Why is 'fear of judgement and rejection' in a chapter about healthy boundaries and advocating for yourself? Some of you might know precisely what it is doing here.

For many autistic and ADHD women, we have spent our lives on a quest to keep everyone else happy. We have worked hard not to let anyone see our struggles.

We've had lifetimes of saying yes when we wanted to say no.

Because of this, the thought of communicating your new boundaries might make you feel anxious and fearful.

The fear is real. Here's the truth: you may lose people along the way. Some people will take longer to accept and respect your boundaries than others. Others will be proud of you and you'll inspire them to follow in your footsteps. And there will be those who will be repelled by your newfound boundaries entirely.

Whilst the pain of people's rejection is hard, trust that those who do not accept or respect your boundaries are not meant to be in your life. You do not need to entertain anyone who refuses to respect your boundaries. When you let those people go, you make way for new connections and relationships to form, where your boundaries are respected.

BURNOUT AND OVERWHELM

When you have no boundaries, you will experience overwhelm and burnout. This might show up as intermittent episodes or you might live in a constant state of anxiety and dread.

I encourage you to get to know your early signs of burnout and overwhelm and have a plan for how to support yourself. Understand when you need to step back and recharge. You will find it much easier to rebalance at the early stages, to avoid a significant, longer-term episode.

Your boundaries are the perfect way to show yourself the respect you deserve, and they will help you avoid being overwhelmed and burnt out.

DISCOVERING YOUR BOUNDARIES

Start with your core values in mind when you choose your boundaries. This will ensure you create the perfect boundaries to advocate from. Remember, your values are your internal guiding compass.

Review your work on your values from Chapter Three and now consider your past experiences.

- Identify moments when you felt uncomfortable, disrespected, ignored or overwhelmed.
- What were the common factors in these situations?
- Think about the people, places and situations you were in.
- Think about all areas of your life, including professional, personal and social perspectives.

- Are there any patterns? For example, is the same person present, the same social or work situation, or a familiar family environment?
- What is most important to you in your personal, social and professional life?

Next, consider your feelings. Discomfort, resentment or frustration often indicate that a boundary has been crossed, as do anger, sadness and disappointment. These emotional signals are your internal compass that will guide you towards understanding your limits.

Then, identify relationships or situations where you felt respected and valued so that you have a comparison. Note down the feelings you experience. What is it about them that made you feel respected and valued? This is a great insight into what healthy boundaries look like for you.

You may benefit from a short break between considering times when you felt respected and times when you didn't. It's called 'breaking state' and can help to move from a focus on negative experiences to positive ones. If you can do this easily and continue your flow then please do so, but if you find it difficult to switch your focus, take a break and come back to the exercise.

Establishing healthy boundaries is an ongoing life process. As your life circumstances change, your boundaries will need to be adjusted.

SETTING YOUR BOUNDARIES

The first step is to be clear on your boundaries and why you have them – the *why* is essential, ultimately, to create a safe, balanced, happy and fulfilling life for yourself. When you know your *why*, you will become more confident in advocating for yourself.

Here are some ideas for healthy boundaries if you need some help.

Professional Boundaries: Examples of professional boundaries could be:

- Decline work meetings outside of your working hours.
- Ask for an agenda before an important meeting so that you can prepare.
- Have allocated breaks in your day to avoid being overwhelmed or have a workspace set up in a way that meets your sensory needs.

Personal Boundaries:

- Decline invitations and requests that you don't want to do or don't have the capacity for.
- Prioritise time for activities that you enjoy.
- Have an hour after work to decompress before you interact with others.

Social Boundaries:

- Limit the frequency of social activities to avoid feeling overwhelmed.
- Express your preferences for small group interactions or one-on-one meet-ups over large gatherings.
- Choose to leave social events early if you feel overwhelmed or exhausted rather than forcing yourself to stay.

Emotional Boundaries:

- Share your feelings openly and ask for help and support when needed.
- Push back against others who invalidate or dismiss your feelings or experiences.
- Start saying 'no' to things you don't feel able to do without detrimental effects on your well-being.

Please remember that how others react to your newfound boundaries is a reflection on *them* and not on you. Ignoring your boundaries shows a lack of respect and care on their part. They may not like that they have lost some perceived control over you. As painful as it can be, it is sometimes best to distance yourself from these people.

You may find yourself questioning whether your boundaries are reasonable when you experience pushback. Remember that your boundaries are there to protect your well-being, improve your experiences and, in some cases, enhance your connections with others.

Only some people are going to like or accept your boundaries. Similarly, you will not necessarily understand other people's boundaries. Understanding and agreeing with someone's boundaries isn't necessary. Respecting them is.

If you find yourself questioning whether your boundaries are 'reasonable', remember why you set them in the first place. They are there to protect your well-being and are an act of self-care and self-respect.

COMMUNICATING YOUR BOUNDARIES

Take a deep breath; this is the part that can feel scary. But you *can* do this!

How you communicate your boundaries will be personal to you. In some cases, you may be open and feel able to communicate with ease. In other cases, you may quietly set your new boundaries by pushing back on a request to meet outside work hours or renegotiating deadlines, for example.

You don't have to come out and tell everyone about your new boundaries unless you want to, in which case, go you!

It will likely feel uncomfortable at first, but the more you do it, the easier it will become. Remember that you will be the one most aware that you are setting boundaries. Other people may not specifically notice that you are starting to say no, renegotiating what is asked of you, or asking for support. The discomfort will likely be yours as you start to change your actions and interactions. It will get more comfortable over time.

Your boundaries will change throughout your life as new situations arise or new people come into your life. When you encounter new situations and people, think from the outset about what you would like these experiences to be like for you. You can then lead with healthy boundaries from the outset.

HOW TO ADVOCATE FOR YOURSELF USING BOUNDARIES

These are some examples of how I set boundaries in different areas of my life. I've shared them to give you real-life insight into how you can choose to approach boundary setting.

Professional Boundary: Honouring Your Time.

Pre-diagnosis, I worked long hours in my skin and scar clinic. I worked through lunch, answered messages outside of work hours and always went above and beyond for my clients. This led to a constant state of stress and anxiety that would result in a couple of big burnouts a year, where I struggled to function.

The New Boundary: I set my work hours and decided I would only be available to work and communicate with clients during those times. I updated my hours on all platforms, created new terms of service and sent them to my clients, new and old. I made three significant changes. First, I set working days and hours. Secondly, I set Out of Office on all platforms, confirming my availability and I didn't respond outside these hours. Thirdly, clients now sign my T&Cs *before* a consultation and treatment to make any issues that may arise easier to resolve.

I felt like a weight was lifted off my shoulders. Since I implemented these changes, I have stuck to my new working pattern and feel much better. It was uncomfortable at first, but now I don't give it any thought, as my terms are agreed upon before a consultation occurs, without any uncomfortable conversations.

Personal Situation: The One-Way Friendship

My friendships had a very clear pattern. I behaved as I believed a friend should. I listened, offered advice and supported wherever possible. The problems arose when I needed my friends to provide the same level of care and support, and they weren't there. I was often left confused, frustrated and hurt.

I knew I needed to create healthy boundaries in my friendships; it was a source of anxiety and upset for me. A situation arose shortly after my diagnosis where I noticed this familiar pattern within a friendship.

I did something I *never* thought I would do. I told them how I felt about how they treated me and that I felt it was *unacceptable*. They responded with a half-hearted apology and a raft of excuses. I suggested coffee to try to resolve the issues and I didn't hear from them again. After the initial hurt had passed, I realised I was better off without this person in my life. They were only in the friendship for what they could gain from it.

These situations can be painful, but you do not need people like this in your life. Let them go; you will make room for true friendships and genuine connections.

My friendships are now based on mutual respect and love, and I feel comfortable expressing my thoughts and emotions.

Social Boundary: Knowing Your Limits

It can be easy to take on too much in social situations, whether it's the frequency of events or the environment.

Maybe you have a friend or group you love to see, but you always meet in noisy bars, restaurants, or pubs. If noisy environments feel like a sensory assault, consider alternative, quieter locations to meet in.

If your friends like to meet regularly, and you struggle to cope with so many social meetups, limit yourself to the ones you genuinely want to go to. Be honest with your friends and tell them you love seeing them, but you also need time to relax and decompress.

I now see my friends in quieter environments and one-on-one rather than in a group. I get to spend quality time with people I love and feel better connected to them. I also show up as me, rather than the version of me I had to be to hide the anxiety and overwhelm.

THE IMPORTANCE OF NEGOTIATION WHEN ADVOCATING FOR YOURSELF

To advocate for your own needs, you need to understand that what is being asked of you doesn't have to be a yes or no. You can negotiate the request so it feels comfortable and aligned for you. To do this, you need to understand how to negotiate. This was a revelation to me, which is ironic given my legal background.

If someone asks you to do something, do you automatically assume your option is to say yes or no?

Here's a couple of scenarios to consider:

1. A friend invites you for drinks at a pub near her house, forty-five minutes from you, on a weekday evening.
2. You are asked to complete a work project by 5 pm the next day, but you won't be able to complete the project unless you work late.

Do you see these as yes/no options?

Or would you negotiate what is being asked of you so that it feels more comfortable and achievable for you?

I believed these were yes/no options and never considered I could negotiate or change the terms. But you *can* negotiate or make suggestions for changes to what is being asked of you. It doesn't have to be a straightforward yes/no answer.

Here's how you could negotiate in the scenarios we just looked at.

1. You tell your friend you'd love to meet her, but it's too far to travel on a work night as you would get in late. Instead, you suggest meeting at a place that is mid-distance between you, or you might suggest meeting on a weekend night instead.

2. You say you'd love to help with the project but can't meet the requested deadline. You communicate it will take three days to complete, or you might ask for additional resources to help you achieve an earlier deadline.

These responses are based on what is realistic, comfortable and achievable to you. They respect your boundaries and needs.

Remember, you can negotiate so that your boundaries are met and respected. Respecting healthy boundaries starts with you; you can choose what you are comfortable with. Life doesn't have to be on others' terms.

WHAT YOU NEED VERSUS WHAT YOU'RE ALLOWED

Your boundaries are about respecting *your* wants and needs and *not* based on what you think others will consider acceptable or reasonable. Remove any thoughts of what you believe you're 'allowed'.

You will meet resistance and some people may try and test you. You'll feel pressure to give in and do what you are asked but stay strong. It may take time for others to get used to your new boundaries and you may have to reinforce them multiple times.

Get comfortable with feeling uncomfortable. Your confidence will grow and eventually, it will feel second nature to you to live your life with your boundaries in place.

ADVOCATE FOR YOURSELF

Advocating for yourself can feel scary. It can help to enlist the support of a partner, friend or colleague you trust. Explain to them that you are making changes for your well-being and ask them to support you. Then, if you feel that someone is not respectful of your boundaries or anxiety creeps in, you have someone with you who can act as backup if needed.

Whilst it might sound silly, practice what you could say in different situations. In the early days, I role-played in my head or practised saying something out loud. It helped me feel more comfortable and familiar with it before I had to say it in real life. Try it and see how you get on.

THE ART OF SAYING NO

Saying 'No' to someone can be tricky. The more you practice, the more you'll get used to it. Over time, it will become easier to say no and to negotiate ways of doing things.

Here are a couple of tips if you're struggling with saying no.

If you're asked to go somewhere you don't want to go, try "Thank you for the invite. I'm not sure if I can make that, but I will check my diary and come back to you later today". Then, you have time to think and respond in a way that feels good for you, whether in person, over the phone, via text or email.

You could also try, "I'm not sure if I can commit to that right now; I'll let you know by X date/time."

Take the pressure off and give yourself space to consider what you'd like to do and how you'd like to respond. It can stop decision anxiety in its tracks and lessen the chances of you saying a hasty yes when you want to say no.

If you feel pressure in the moment to say yes, or you're with a person who pushes your boundaries, then the above techniques can help. You also have the opportunity to respond in a way that you're comfortable with, for example, via email or text, rather than over the phone or in person. When you remove the ability for someone to apply pressure in the moment, you have control over the situation and your response.

BEING IN CONTROL

I have lived my life in a constant state of anxiety that if I didn't do everything asked of me, people wouldn't like me; they would reject me and think I was useless. I over-delivered every time, hoping it would make them like me more.

After my diagnosis, I had a conversation with a coach about boundaries. It dawned on me that I had *never* considered them.

Not only was it a huge revelation to learn that I could create boundaries and negotiate what was asked of me, but there were also some shocking discoveries and realisations to come.

I could see where others had taken advantage of me over the years. Whilst I felt empowered, I also felt sadness and shame that I allowed myself to be treated in this way. I started viewing situations and people differently and noticed who supported me and who were only in it for themselves.

As I introduced healthy boundaries into my life, there were significant shifts in how I worked and interacted with people.

I let a lot of people go from my life who had taken advantage of me. I felt like I was losing everyone around me whilst I found my true self. It was a surreal experience.

Whilst the initial few months were scary, I can now say it's the best thing I ever did for myself. My anxiety levels are much lower and I feel calmer and happier than I ever have. I never apologise for my boundaries because I know it's an act of self-respect and love.

I don't shout my boundaries from the rooftops; I just mindfully live by them daily. I am confident to push back when I feel they are not being respected and I am happy to step away from people and situations that do not feel good for me. For the first time, I feel in control.

SUMMARY

We have covered the importance of creating and maintaining healthy boundaries. You've learned about the benefits of having healthy boundaries and the consequences of not having them.

We've looked at how you can discover boundaries that are right for you and how you can communicate them to others.

If you find it hard to say no, I've shared some tips on how to buy yourself some time to remove the stress and pressure.

With these insights and tools, you'll now see how important it is to set your life up to support you so you can live on your terms. Healthy boundaries are a key component of this, enabling you to live life on your terms and stop putting everyone else's needs before yours.

Remember, your boundaries are a sign of self-respect. They set the benchmark for what you will and won't tolerate. When you connect with others, ensuring your relationship is built on mutual respect for each other's boundaries is crucial.

With your new healthy boundaries in mind, let us move on to the next chapter, where you're going to learn how to transform your life.

TOP FIVE TAKE-AWAYS

1. Healthy boundaries are not selfish but a sign of self-respect and love.
2. Healthy boundaries are essential to your well-being.
3. Healthy boundaries help to protect you against being overwhelmed and burnt out.
4. You are allowed to say 'no', and you can negotiate what is being asked of you.
5. Create boundaries based on your values, needs and wants, not what you believe you are allowed or what others will consider acceptable.

7

TRANSFORMING YOUR LIFE

You now have the tools to create a life where balance, happiness, fulfilment and a sense of achievement coexist. This chapter shows you how to use those tools to transform your life.

You can now create a version of happiness and success that feels good for *you* and ignores societal expectations. You do not have to determine success by the outward standards shown in the media; *you* can choose what success means. And, more importantly, you get to live in a way that feels safe and supported, where you feel accepted, understood and valued. Your life, your way.

This chapter will help you bring all the previous steps of RADIATE together, so it becomes your reality.

BRINGING IT ALL TOGETHER

It takes patience and commitment to get to know and be honest with yourself on a deeper level. It takes courage to face the parts you have hidden away or felt ashamed of and to see them through a new, non-judgemental lens. I hope you're proud of yourself and how far you've come.

Now is the time to take action. You need to put into practice all that you have learnt to create the life you want to live. Without action, nothing will change.

You didn't come this far, to only come this far, did you? I didn't think so!

VALUES AND GOALS

Remember, it *all* comes back to your core values. If you rushed through Chapter Four, please revisit it. If you aren't clear on your *true* core values, the whole RADIATE model falls apart and you are doing yourself a huge disservice. Your values are your internal compass and they will guide you in your decisions and choices. Take the time to make sure you choose values that you deeply connect with and envisage living by.

Try this: When faced with a decision, ask yourself, "Is this aligned with my values?". Draw on the exercises from Chapter Four, where you focused on what being in and out of alignment felt like. The more you practice being consciously aware, the easier this will become and you will naturally start to make choices based on your values.

Your goals and vision for the future are also essential guides. It is easy to become side-tracked or distracted. Revisit them often to stay aligned. When working towards goals, don't look for perfection with every action; the quest for perfection can hinder us and procrastination can creep in. Instead, ask yourself whether your choices are 'directionally correct'. I learnt the term directionally correct from my business mentor, Daniel Priestley, and it immediately impacted how I approached my choices and decisions as I let go of the need for perfection.

When directionally correct, you make decisions moving towards your goals and desires. The actions don't need to be perfect but must move you in the right direction. Imperfect action is better than no action!

VISION BOARD REVISITED

You created your life vision in Chapter Two. Now I want you to revisit it with fresh eyes.

Consider your vision board or life story vision (or however you chose to record your life vision) alongside everything you have discovered since you created it. Make any changes you want to ensure that each area of your life enables you to live a happy and fulfilled life on your terms. Review your vision regularly. Your vision isn't set in stone, you can make whatever changes you want or need to make to remain aligned.

You can also use your vision board or life story vision to see if a choice or decision is directionally correct. It can shine a spotlight on a decision that may help you achieve a goal in one area of your life but pull you away from another area.

For example, you may have a work opportunity requiring longer hours. It will help you with your professional goals, but you'll have less time with your family and one of your family goals is to be home for dinner every night. You can use your vision board as a guide to decide whether the work opportunity is right for you. You may feel that the short-term sacrifice to achieve your overall life vision is worth it. Or you may decide not to pursue the work opportunity because family time is your top priority. Alternatively (this is important), you may get creative and find ways to balance the work opportunity and your family life, perhaps by asking for support, negotiating deadlines or requesting days working from home. Remember, you *can* negotiate life on your terms.

Another example could be that you have been invited to participate in a six-month leadership program, which means you will be away from home Monday to Friday. This program is renowned for enhancing leadership skills and expanding professional networks, which aligns perfectly with your goals for career development and progression. However, one of your core values is connection and you know that time away from home will impact your personal relationships. You can consider the opportunity against your vision board and be guided by your core values. You may decide that this opportunity is too good to miss, or you may choose to decline the offer. Also, think about where there might be a compromise solution. Perhaps you could arrange in advance for friends and family to visit you whilst you're away or set up regular video calls with them. Or you could ask whether it's possible to attend some of the course remotely, via video link.

Your vision board doesn't have to be photos; you can write things down or record them on voice notes. Just remember to check in with it regularly. I recommend monthly for the first six months if you haven't used one before, then, every three months or when any big life events come up.

MAKING MAGIC HAPPEN

 *NEWSFLASH*
You need to take action to make changes in your life.

The thought of change is scary, but life will stay the same if you don't take action and make positive changes. You made it to Chapter Seven, which tells me you *want to* change your life to feel happy, calm and fulfilled.

The choice, as always, is yours.

Get comfortable with being uncomfortable in the short term whilst you create and build the life you want to live in a way that feels good for you.

Or you can *choose* to make no changes and continue as you are. You can continue as a prolific people-pleaser, living on everyone else's terms and constantly being overwhelmed, burnt out and miserable.

You have all that you need to create the life you truly desire. You *can* do this. My advice is to start small and find ways to make manageable changes. Think about where you could start to use your strengths daily. Try the techniques for saying no to things you don't want to do that we looked at in Chapter Six.

Please let go of the need for perfection. You do not need to take perfect action, just action. You can try different ways of doing things; if they don't work for you, let them go and try something else. Your confidence will grow and your momentum will build with each action you take. I'd highly recommend James Clear's book, *Atomic Habits*[14]; it is excellent for helping build new habits gradually.

Write your core values down and keep them somewhere you can see them daily. They will serve as a reminder each time you see them and help them to become ingrained in your memory.

Write a list of your strengths so you have a reminder of what you're good at and use them as prompts for daily action. Focus on small ways you can maximise your strengths every day. Remember that when you focus on your strengths, it helps to improve your sense of achievement, fulfilment, and confidence.

Have your vision board somewhere prominent as a reminder of the life you are creating for yourself. If your board is visual, put it on a wall you regularly walk past or as the screen saver on your laptop.

---

14. James Clear, *Atomic Habits. Tiny Changes, Remarkable Results.* October 2018.

MAKING THE LEAP

Now, it is time to take action! I want you to come up with three to five actions that you can take in the next week. Here are some examples to get you started.

- Commit to using one of your core strengths daily and find new ways to use it.
- Say no to something you don't want to do or negotiate what's been asked so that it works for you.
- Automate, delegate or eliminate something in your life.
- Ask for help or support from a colleague, friend, partner or family member.

These are just ideas; you can choose your actions, but you need to take *some* action.

EXAMPLES/CASE STUDIES

Here are a couple of life examples that may resonate with you. We will look at life before and after implementing the RADIATE model so you can see the difference it can make.

Meet Emma

Emma, 41, ran a thriving marketing business. She was married and a mum to two children. She'd been in business for three years and, whilst she loved what she did, she constantly felt overwhelmed and out of control. She had so much work on, her desk was always a mess and her accounts were in disarray. She lived in fear of her accounts being audited.

Emma worked long hours, felt guilty that she wasn't there for her family as much as she'd like and felt like she was letting her partner and children down. Emma lay in bed at night worrying and woke up exhausted and drained. Even though she was struggling, she volunteered to help at school events and attended every work occasion she was invited to. She also socialised with her husband and their friends. She said yes to everything because she didn't want anyone to feel let down or think she couldn't cope. Her fear of not being good enough meant she always over-delivered.

After RADIATE

Emma got clear on her values, passions and vision for her life and realised that she wasn't living in alignment with any of the important things to her. She discovered a disconnect between who she truly was and her life. Her vision board highlighted that family was incredibly important to her. Yet she had created a business that took her away from her family, so she couldn't be present with them.

Emma loved her work and described it as her dream job. She was passionate about helping her clients but realised that her business was running her and not the other way around.

Emma made two big decisions; the first was to create set working hours for herself, allowing her to have dinner with her family every night and spend weekends with her children. She also took ADE (automate, delegate, and eliminate) to heart. As a result, she brought in a PA and accountant, which helped her to automate and delegate a large proportion of the administrative work. This took a lot of pressure off and freed up a significant amount of time.

Emma's professional life became more balanced, so she focused on her personal life. She explained to her husband and children that she needed their help at home. They shared household tasks and Emma let go of the need for perfection and embraced the concept of 'good enough'. She accepted that she was not a failure if things weren't perfect.

With friendships and social events, Emma withdrew from the school parents' committee and accepted she didn't have time to organise school events. She distanced herself from friends who drained her of her time and energy and spent time with friends she felt relaxed and happy with. She started to limit her social activities and went to the ones she genuinely wanted to go to.

Every choice and decision was made with her values and goals at heart. She fell back into old habits on occasions in the early days but quickly recognised that and learned from it. The small changes led to bigger ones, and Emma now feels more balanced and happier. The help she brought in for her business has allowed her to focus on what she's good at and she continues to go from strength to strength without over-stretching herself.

Meet Stevie, Age 37

After a decade as a marketing executive, Stevie resigned from her corporate job as she felt limited and suffocated. She started her business as a brand consultant from a small home office. The initial phase was challenging, with long hours, difficulties securing clients and no real plan or strategy for her business. Stevie loved the freedom and creativity of her work, but after the first year, she felt overwhelmed and out of control. She didn't see her friends anymore and began to think she'd made a huge mistake leaving her corporate job.

After RADIATE

Stevie was at a point where she was considering closing her business and finding what she called 'a real job'.

Stevie's most significant revelation came quickly. She realised that many of her decisions, choices and beliefs did not come from her but from others. She had accepted what others said she 'should' be doing and how. And when someone close to her said she needed a real job, she interpreted that as her business was not 'real' or viable.

Stevie was on a journey and slowly making the changes she needed to move her towards the life she wanted to lead. While working out exactly what she wanted, she focused on areas where she could implement change immediately.

To transform her life, she introduced some fundamental changes.

As with Emma, she established set working hours to protect her well-being and avoid burnout and overwhelm. Stevie also took on a virtual assistant to organise her workload and manage her diary. These two things created more time for Stevie to focus on business growth.

She stopped trying to create a business based on what everyone else told her she 'should' do or what other similar businesses did. She focused on honing her unique skills and talents and carving her path. She committed to showing up with authenticity and letting her personality shine through, which attracted clients she loved to work with.

Stevie also learned to prioritise and say no to invitations and opportunities that did not align with her values and goals. This was tough for her, but she reminded herself that her boundaries were about self-respect, which helped her put her needs first.

Only a year into her business, Stevie was unclear on her overall vision for her life as she adapted to life as an entrepreneur. Now, she has achieved more balance and is committed to finding her version of success and creating life on her terms. Her vision board and core values will be her guides as she progresses on her path.

WHOLE LIFE, PART LIFE AND SITUATIONAL

My RADIATE model will always meet you exactly where you're at, and you can use it to transform your whole life, individual areas of your life or specific situations.

I ask myself these questions, no matter the circumstances:

- What is happening for me right now?
- What am I thinking, feeling, experiencing?
- What choice or decision will be directionally correct for the life I want to live (goals/vision)?
- Does this align with my core values?
- Does this play to my strengths?
- Do I have the capacity to do this right now?
- Is this something I want and am comfortable with?
- What do I need at this moment? Do I need some support?
- Do I want to say yes?

It might take a few days to work through if it's a more significant life decision. It may only take a few minutes to decide if a situation needs an immediate answer. The important thing is that you always return to what feels good for you and you respect and protect your needs and wants.

A NEW PERSON

It's impossible to articulate the mammoth transformation I have experienced since my autism and ADHD diagnosis and going through and creating my RADIATE model. I barely recognise the person I was before. I will continue to evolve and grow, using my RADIATE model to guide me.

These days, I opt for a calm life that leaves me feeling energised and fulfilled rather than forcing myself to do what others expect from me.

There are no late-night parties, no noisy bars and no time spent mediating the dramas of others.

I know my true self and am proud of who I am. I understand and accept all parts of me and I have built my life around this. There's no more judgement or shame.

To the outside world, my life might seem unremarkable. Many bystanders might struggle to see my changes and how different my life is. But the difference is in how I *feel* and the quality of my life experiences. Feeling out of control, on the edge of burnout and in a state of permanent anxiety has been replaced with calm, clarity and a sense of balance. I have developed my own version of what achievement and success mean for me, letting go of the societal expectations I had pursued for so long. My prolific people-pleasing and fear of rejection, judgement, and unworthiness have been replaced by an inner strength and desire to look after and respect myself, knowing I am worthy. I've let go of the desire to be perfect and replaced it with an acceptance that 'good enough' is enough. I know I am enough, and I've stopped trying to prove that to anyone else. And I have replaced the shame and feelings of being broken I have carried for decades with pride and confidence that I am different, not less, and that I, like you, am extraordinary in my unique way.

SUMMARY

In this chapter, you have discovered how to bring the previous steps of my RADIATE model to life.

You've learnt that you must make changes to create the life you truly want. It will be uncomfortable sometimes but, by starting with minor changes, you will build your confidence and make more significant changes over time. Remember that the tiny changes are the ones that can lead to more significant changes.

You've seen how Emma and Stevie transformed their lives and whilst it might not look so different to the outside world, it dramatically changed their experiences and how they felt inside.

Your vision for the future may be entirely different from where you are right now, or you may only need to make a few changes to align yourself. Perhaps you're like Stevie and may not yet have clarity around your vision for the long-term future. That's okay; through consistent small actions, you can create the life you want and adapt and adjust as you go.

Use my RADIATE model to help you in each area. It will always meet you where you're at.

If you're not convinced you can make the changes you want, wait until you've read the next chapter. You'll be ready to jump in headfirst after that.

TOP FIVE TAKE-AWAYS

1. You must take action to make change happen.
2. Revisiting your vision board ensures you stay aligned with your goals and vision.
3. Choose three to five small actions you can take this week.
4. You can use RADIATE to transform your life, individual areas or specific situations.
5. You always have a choice. Making no choice is a choice.

8

EMPOWER

We've come to the final step of the RADIATE model and for me, a very precious one – Empower. In the model, empower has a dual meaning. Firstly, it's about feeling empowered to take action and create the life you want unapologetically. Secondly, it's about how you empower other women like you and future generations of neurodivergent girls to do the same.

I'll share my vision and mission for the future and how you can be part of an incredible movement to smash apart outdated stereotypes. You'll discover how you can be a catalyst for change so that younger generations of neurodivergent girls don't relive the challenges many of us have.

You'll learn powerful ways to communicate your diagnosis to others to improve your life experiences and connections. And you'll learn how *you* are an inspiring role model for others.

By the end of this chapter, you'll have a fire lit inside of you and feel prepared to go out into the world as your true, authentic, and extraordinary self. Your newfound knowledge of the wider impact you can have will spur you on to be brave and unapologetic as you create a life on *your* terms.

BE EMPOWERED AND EMPOWER OTHERS

Your empowerment is about having the confidence to act and live your life in a way that ensures you feel safe, supported, happy and fulfilled. In today's world, it is easy to succumb to the pressure to live and act in a way that is expected of us or deemed acceptable to other people. It is human nature to copy others and so, patterns of behaviour evolve, and society expects us to all act the same. It has been scientifically proven[15] that we copy others, even when it's incorrect or irrational; it is part of our evolutionary wiring to belong.

When you feel empowered, you resist the pressure to conform to societal standards of success and happiness and you choose to carve your path in the world unapologetically.

The knock-on effect of *your* living a fulfilled and happy life, boldly and confidently, is that you show other women what they can achieve, and you become the person that shines a spotlight on a different way. You show them that they don't need to try to compromise and sacrifice themselves to fit in. It becomes a domino effect; the more we do this, the more inspiring role models we create. We give both this generation and generations to come a different perspective and narrative, and together, we dismantle and destroy the outdated

---

15. https://greatergood.berkeley.edu/article/item/why_imitation_is_at_the_heart_of_being_human

stereotypes that have suffocated and held us back for too long.

MY MISSION AND VISION

When I was diagnosed as autistic and ADHD in my mid-forties, my initial plan wasn't to write this book or set up The Autistic Joyologist. The catalyst for doing both came from my experiences post-diagnosis, as I tried to improve my life experiences and 'fit in' to society.

As I searched for support and ways to make changes, I struggled to find solutions that resonated with me. This was coupled with multiple people rejecting my diagnosis, as I didn't fit the version of what being autistic or ADHD 'looked' like. I lost friends and, as months passed by, I began to panic that my diagnosis had come too late in life.

That's why I am working with women like you, neurodivergent women, women who have always felt a bit 'different', who want to step into a life that feels like it's yours rather than fighting to live a life you believe you *should* live. Deep down, you know that you have compromised and sacrificed your true self for too long, and you're not going to do it any longer. You want to realise your potential and live in a way that feels aligned to you, whatever that might be.

You're ready to show up and do life your way, without the self-sacrifice and compromise that's hung over you to this point.

I know that, together, we can be a powerful catalyst for change that reshapes the narrative of what being neurodivergent 'looks' like, especially for females. Together, we can smash outdated stereotypes, remove stigmas and ensure our future generations lead happy and thriving lives in a society that better understands and accepts them.

SOME EYE-OPENING FACTS

I wanted to share some specific facts that stuck with me during my research. Some of these had me in tears, some made me smile and others made me angry and frustrated. If you're still sitting on the fence about empowering others, then these statistics will be a powerful motivator. There's a balance between negative and positive. All highlight the desperate need for a societal shift in how many autistic and ADHD individuals are perceived and treated.

- Nearly 80% of autistic women are misdiagnosed with a mental health condition or personality disorder[16]. Some are never diagnosed autistic; if they are, it's later in life.

- Recent research shows that on average, females are diagnosed in their thirties and forties, while males are seven[17]. Females typically have a longer diagnosis delay after they first present to the medical health service.

- There remains a gender bias in diagnostic criteria and assessment tools, which continues to contribute to many females being overlooked.[18] From the inception of the diagnostic tools, there has been significant gender bias and this has still not been rectified at the time of writing.

---

16. https://www.durham.ac.uk/research/current/thought–leadership/women–with–autism—adhd–arent–diagnosed–until–adulthood/

17. https://www.thebraincharity.org.uk/neurodivergent–women–adhd–autism–adults/

18. https://autism.org/women–in–autism/

Of course, we will not look solely at negative statistics, although sadly, I have a plethora of those. Here are some more positive ones to consider:

- Research shows that you are 500% more likely to be an entrepreneur if you have ADHD.[19] Your wonderful neurodivergent brain gives you a distinct edge in being an entrepreneur.

- Those neurodivergent traits that you might consider problematic can be your strengths in business. Risk-taking and impulsivity can be your greatest attributes. Combined with your unique perspectives and skills, you have a perfect recipe for success. I'd recommend you read an amazing article in ADDitude Magazine called *Entrepreneurship and ADHD: Fast Brain, Fast Company*.[20]

- There are *huge* wins to be had from a neurodiverse team in business. Hewlett Packard reported that neurodiverse teams were 30% more productive, and The Harvard Business Review reported 19% more profitability for organisations that actively promote inclusivity in their workforce.[21]

There's a clear disconnect between these two sets of facts and statistics for women. We face challenges of late diagnosis, misdiagnosis and gender bias, yet our unique neurodivergent brains clearly give us a business advantage.

---

19. Understanding the Strong Connection Between Entrepreneurs and ADHD– FastBraiin

20. Neurodiversity Is a Competitive Advantage (hbr.org)

21. https://makeadifference.media/culture/spotlight–on–the–benefits–of–neurodiverse–teams/

The way forward is to stop hiding and trying to fit in and to become empowered to stand out and showcase what we can achieve with authenticity.

SMASHING APART OUTDATED STEREOTYPES

Despite the increased awareness of autism and ADHD in recent years, society still has outdated stereotypes. Females are still assessed and diagnosed based on criteria that are biased towards males 'and the support offered is woefully inadequate, in my opinion.

Above, we saw that females are eighty per cent more likely to be diagnosed with a mental health condition rather than autism or ADHD. [22] It is frightening to consider that many women have been prescribed medication for conditions they do not have.

Neither ADHD nor autism are 'young male' conditions, which is still the basis that the diagnostic criteria in the UK are based on. As a society, we must step away from these stereotypes and take time to understand and accept others' experiences, even where they don't fit with an idea we have in our minds.

The reason so many women receive a late diagnosis, or no diagnosis at all, is because of these stereotypes. It is because we present *nothing* like a young male, or white, middle-to-upper-class young male, to be precise.

You can be a catalyst for significant change in this area through living an aligned and happy life.

---

22. https://www.durham.ac.uk/research/current/thought–leadership/women–with–autism––adhd–arent–diagnosed–until–adulthood/

EMPOWERING OTHER WOMEN AND FUTURE GENERATIONS

Together, we can empower ourselves, each other and future generations. I know you will have experienced struggles and challenges, and I know that, like me, you've had enough.

You're ready to live on *your* terms and stop trying to fit into a society that was not designed for you. You're ready to be bold, courageous and unapologetic as you create a life that leaves you fulfilled and happy.

You are now empowered to take control and let your extraordinary talents shine. Your actions *will* inspire others to follow in your footsteps, like a beautiful domino effect. The legacy impact of your actions today will become a catalyst for change so that future generations can thrive, not hide.

SHARING A DIAGNOSIS

It's important to talk about how you share your autism, ADHD or other neurodivergence with others. I am talking about both clinical and self-diagnosis here. You can feel empowered to live your best life, but an unexpected response to a shared diagnosis can derail some of us.

I want you to feel empowered, especially when someone challenges you or you receive a response you don't expect.

This approach shifted my mindset and improved my experiences of sharing my diagnosis immeasurably.

Consider your reason for sharing your diagnosis and what you need the other person(s) to understand. Think about the following:

1. Why are you sharing? Is it because you need additional support or adjustments or because you want to ensure that you communicate effectively with the other person(s)?

2. Let the other person(s) know what you need from them or what you want them to understand about how your autism, ADHD or other neurodivergence impact you.

3. Be honest and open about any adjustments or support you need and don't apologise for them.

Remember, many people that you share your autism and ADHD with will have a limited understanding of what they are. They certainly won't know how *your* autism and ADHD impact you or what you need. Being clear and communicating your unique experiences and needs will ensure that others understand and support you effectively. It takes the guesswork out and makes it easier for everyone involved.

It's important to note that someone's first response might not be their last. Give them time to process what you have shared with them. If you have any resources you can share with them, that can be helpful. You likely needed time to understand your diagnosis and neurodivergent self, so appreciate they may require some time, too.

CREATING A MOVEMENT

This is what gets me out of bed in the morning; it's my passion.

Whether professionally or personally, when you take control of your life and live boldly and unapologetically, you show others that they can do the same. You become a catalyst for change by being your authentic self. You showcase the unique talents and skills you have that neurotypical minds do not possess. You celebrate that you're different, not less.

You may not know it, but you are an inspiration to someone. People will see you and believe they can achieve great things. The narrative around autism and ADHD *will* change and *you* will be a part of that movement.

Imagine the next generation of autistic and ADHD girls showing up boldly, with a belief they can create fulfilling and happy lives on their terms without suffocating or suppressing their true selves.

I previously shared with you the young girls who bravely spoke on Naga Munchetty's BBC Radio 5 Live interview before me, where they spoke of their anxiety and fear of being their true selves and of how they hid who they were to try to fit in with their friends. I shared the horrendous statistic that 70–80% of autistic children are bullied…

Now, imagine being a part of changing their futures by educating society about the real lived experiences of neuro-divergent females. Imagine a society that celebrates neurodiversity and understands and accepts everyone for who they are. Imagine a society where it's not a struggle to fit in where we, as neurodivergent women, belong and feel supported…

You did that. *You.* By taking bold actions to create life on your terms. You are part of the movement to create a more inclusive society for future generations. Feels pretty good, right?

SHOWCASE WHAT'S POSSIBLE!

A neurodivergent brain means you experience and process things differently. Your neurodivergent mind enables you to bring new perspectives and value to the world; you are brilliant.

When you embrace your strengths and create a supportive environment around you, you can harness your skills and talents and achieve your full potential in whichever way you want. You become a force for good when you claim your right to live in a society where you aren't afraid to be your true self. You showcase that society *can* make the adjustments necessary to create a more inclusive and supportive environment for its neurodiverse community with guidance from you and women like you.

SPEAK AUTHENTICALLY AND UNAPOLOGETICALLY

Please don't ever apologise for how your neurodivergent brain works and the support you need. Saying 'I'm sorry' if you ask for accommodation or support is unnecessary. Share your experiences. Share your achievements, your skills, and the positive experiences you have. Share your challenges and difficulties and be open about the support and accommodations you need to ensure you have the best experiences possible.

I encourage you to be as authentic as you share while being proud of all that you are. Human experiences are messy, unique and complicated. When we show up authentically, others will follow in our footsteps. Shared experiences create better understanding, acceptance and connections.

BE AN INSPIRING ROLE MODEL

You will inspire others, even if you don't realise it. Other neurodivergent women will be inspired by your actions and how you show up. Young neurodivergent girls will see all that you achieve and will see what's possible for them.

Your actions and success will be the rocket fuel and inspiration for the next generations to believe they can live a life without limits and constant self-sacrifice. They will be more confident, bold, brave and authentic than our generation because they have seen what is possible.

TOGETHER WE ARE STRONGER

My journey through diagnosis, self-discovery and acceptance was hard. I'd best describe it as a roller coaster. I had the highs of understanding myself fully and developing self-compassion. I had the lows of grieving a life I could have had if I had known sooner and sadness for the way I'd constantly berated myself for not being good enough. I was hit with the harsh realisation that society did not truly understand autism and ADHD, particularly in females, and even less so in females who were already considered successful by societal standards.

I had to deal with people in my life rejecting my diagnosis and being constantly compared to the stereotype of the young boys that the diagnostic criteria are based on. To many, my degree, my career and my success as an entrepreneur meant I couldn't be autistic or have ADHD. The fact I didn't have a monotone voice or lack empathy was another strike in the box, alongside the absence of physical fidgeting.

A few months post-diagnosis, I watched a BBC television program called *Inside Our Autistic Minds*, a documentary with Chris Packham[23], in which he spent time with individuals who were autistic. It had a profound effect on me. In particular, I was struck by an interview in episode one, where they shared statistics that non-intellectually impacted autistic women were eight times more likely to attempt suicide than women who were not autistic. That hit me like a sledgehammer. I was diagnosed with general anxiety disorder at eighteen and had experienced two episodes in my life where I didn't feel I could go on. It felt raw. I felt a mix of sadness and anger as I realised that things may have been different if I had received an earlier diagnosis.

As I reflected, I had an overwhelming realisation that my experiences could have been avoided. These thoughts stuck in my head:

- Life wouldn't have been so hard if society had better understood autism and ADHD, especially in females.

- The stereotypes need to be replaced with acceptance and understanding of the vast experiences of neurodivergent people and their uniqueness.

- Society needs to adapt to support neurodivergent individuals and stop trying to force us to act in a more neurotypical way.

---

23. https://www.bbc.co.uk/iplayer/episode/p0bbnjvx/inside–our–autistic–minds–series–1–episode–1

- There needs to be a greater understanding that being neurodivergent means different, not less. Neurodiversity is a fundamental and necessary part of the human species, and it's time for society to support *all* of us.

- Our next generations must not repeat the experiences I have had. There is no need.

My heart breaks at the thought of younger generations reliving my experiences – a life spent feeling that I never belonged and that I was somehow broken, the bullying I endured, the difficulties with friends and relationships and the constant 'square peg, round hole' situations that arose during my time in corporate.

In real life, I am quiet, introverted, and extremely private. However, I knew that to make a difference in the lives of others and ensure history doesn't repeat itself, I had to speak up and share my story. I knew this was the way to connect with other women like you and that together, we can become inspiring role models to show generations to come what's possible as someone who is autistic and has ADHD. We get to catalyse change and inspire others to follow in our footsteps. We can showcase that being neurodivergent brings incredible gifts and talents that the world needs. Being neurodivergent is part of the richness of neurodiversity, so necessary for the human species.

Courage is one of my core values, and stepping out as The Autistic Joyologist has taken more courage than I knew I had in me. To be seen and heard feels incredibly vulnerable and is the opposite of the decades I've spent hidden away, but I'm doing it. Sometimes, it is hard, but it's worth it if I can make a positive difference in even one person's life.

Thank you for being part of this journey with me. Together, we are stronger.

SUMMARY

The Empower element of RADIATE is the one that often reduces me to tears. It is at the heart of my decision to step out as The Autistic Joyologist, and that is why you are reading this book.

I want you to feel empowered to create a successful and happy life, knowing your actions will empower other women. Go out there and live the life you deserve to live, boldly and unapologetically.

You've learnt how to share a diagnosis with purpose and to never apologise for your needs and the way your beautiful neurodivergent mind works.

You've discovered that when you show up and showcase your talents, you're creating shifts in the narrative of what being autistic and ADHD mean and 'looks' like. You're a catalyst for change and part of a movement to create a better future for future generations.

Because of you, other women will feel empowered to transform their lives, and future generations of autistic and ADHD females will be saved from many of the struggles that we have endured.

Thank you, from the bottom of my heart.

TOP FIVE TAKE-AWAYS

1. The outdated stereotypes have got to go and must be replaced by a deep understanding and acceptance of each person's experience.
2. By creating a happy and successful life on your terms, you inspire others to do the same.
3. When you're sharing your neurodivergence with others, remember why you are sharing it and what you need the other person to know.
4. Never apologise for your neurodivergent mind and the support and accommodations you need.
5. Know that someone, somewhere, is watching you as you showcase what's possible. You inspire someone, even if you don't know it.

CONGRATULATIONS!

Congratulations! You've completed the RADIATE model and now have actionable steps to create a life aligned with your values, vision and goals.

Through the RADIATE exercises, you've uncovered powerful knowledge to move your life forward positively.

A quick reminder of what you have learned in the RADIATE model:

Reflection: You've reflected on your life, past and present. You've defined your vision for the future and what success means for you.

Acceptance: You are clear about your strengths and challenges; you accept your attributes without judgement and have released the desire to change them. You learnt how to maximise your strengths and increase your confidence and happiness.

Discover: You are connected to your core values and understand what living an aligned life looks and feels like for you. You know how to use your values as your internal compass.

Innovate: You created unique strategies to support yourself in challenging areas by focusing on *your* wants and needs.

Advocate: You have created healthy boundaries in your life, and you understand why boundaries are crucial to your well-being. You can confidently ask for the support or accommodations you need to ensure you feel comfortable without an apology.

Transform: You have identified clear action that you can take immediately to move you towards the life you desire. You clearly understand that to transform your life, you must take action, and you now have the tools and confidence you need to do so.

Empower: You feel empowered to make the changes you need and want in your life boldly and unapologetically. You are inspired to empower other women to transform their lives and to become a role model for generations of autistic and ADHD girls.

Your success and happiness are rooted in knowing, respecting and honouring your true self, with your core values at the heart of it all. As your vision for your life evolves and your goals and dreams change, always return to your values and let them be your internal compass.

Use RADIATE as often as you need, and remember, it will always meet you exactly where you are, whether you are going through a big life change, dealing with challenges in an area of your life, or having a specific challenge to over-come.

You now know that the secret to your happiness and success is not to make your brain more 'normal' or neurotypical. It is about mastering your unique ways of thinking and being. Then, you will thrive. In a supportive and calm environment, you can let go of societal expectations and demands and choose a path that plays to your strengths and talents.

You do not have to be perfect; aim to be directionally correct in your actions and choices.

Be brilliant, bold, authentic and unapologetic in your actions, knowing that you will transform your life and inspire all who witness your greatness.

It's time to live your best life on your terms. It's time to stop hiding and start thriving.

I'm excited about your new life. Now, go live it!

STAY IN TOUCH

Thank you for your commitment and hard work throughout this book.

If you're interested in finding out how we can continue to work together to create a life of balance, fulfilment and happiness, I'd love to share the finer details of how you can achieve the life you want and deserve.

Visit – www.autisticjoyologist.co.uk

You'll discover additional resources to support you, including my Permission To Be Different Signature program, alongside other online courses and mini-series.

Email – hello@autisticjoyologist.co.uk

Follow me on social media – @autisticjoyologist

Connect with me on LinkedIn – nikkibutlerautisticjoyologist

REFERENCES/BIBLIOGRAPHY

Chapter One

Indiana University. (2015, March 26). Stereotypes
	lower math performance in women, but effects
	go unrecognized. *ScienceDaily*. Retrieved
	December 29, 2023, from www.sciencedaily.com/
	releases/2015/03/150326162600.htm

Dr Alokananda Rudra, 'Why many women with autism and
	ADHD aren't diagnosed until adulthood – and what to
	do if you think you're one of them' Durham University
	Blog (22 April 2022)

https://www.durham.ac.uk/research/current/
	thought-leadership/women-with-autism-adhd-arent-
	diagnosed-until-adulthood/, accessed 22 October 2023

Chapter Two

How to create a vision board, Nikki Butler– The Autistic
	Joyologist YouTube https://youtu.be/6xzZjDzW3SE

Chapter Three

Nancy Doyle, Neurodiversity at work: a biopsychosocial model and the impact on working adults, British Medical Bulletin, Volume 135, Issue 1, September 2020, Pages 108–125, https://doi.org/10.1093/bmb/ldaa021

Brene Brown, 'Do Not Negotiate Who You Are' (2023) https://youtu.be/EI89XK2L6I4 accessed 24 April 2023

Xie H. 'Strengths-based approach for mental health recovery'. *National Library of Medicine,* Iran J Psychiatry Behav Sci. 2013 Fall;7(2):5-10. PMID: 24644504; PMCID: PMC3939995. https://www.ncbi.nlm.nih.gov/pmc/articles/PMC3939995/ accessed 23 November 2023

Robert D. Austin and Gary P. Pisano 'Neurodiversity as a Competitive Advantage – Why you should embrace it in your workforce'. *Harvard Business Review magazine* May-June 2017, accessed 14 August 2023. https://hbr.org/2017/05/neurodiversity-as-a-competitive-advantage

Chapter Four

Dean Graziosi Seven Layers Deep worksheet and example

https://www.deangraziosi.com/wp-content/uploads/2021/03/7-Levels-Deep-Exercise.pdf

Danielle La Porte *'The Firestarter Sessions'* 18 February 2014 https://www.audible.co.uk/pd/The-Fire-Starter-Sessions-Audiobook/B007SY96II, accessed 20 February 2014

Elizabeth Gilbert, *'Big Magic'* 22 September 2016. https://www.audible.co.uk/pd/Big-Magic-Audiobook/B012YGQ5PG, accessed 29 September 2016

Chapter Five

Xie H. Strengths-based approach for mental health recovery. *National Library of Medicine* Iran J Psychiatry Behav Sci. 2013 Fall;7(2):5–10. PMID: 24644504; PMCID: PMC3939995. https://www.ncbi.nlm.nih.gov/pmc/articles/PMC3939995/, accessed 12 June 2023

Impact (author unknown) 'Benefits of a Strength-Based Approach' 26 January 2023 Work With Impact website, https://workwithimpact.co.uk/news/benefits-of-a-strength-based-approach/ accessed 21 September 2023

Jason Stephenson *'Spoken Meditation: Your Ideal Life, The Law Of Attraction: Goal Setting Visualization'* 2014 https://youtu.be/J11_JxqSJlE?si=h1t7oqJueURorkYl accessed April 2020

Chapter Six

Helen Thompson, 'Why emotions can feel so painful – and what it means for painkillers' *New Scientist,* 16 November 2022, https://www.newscientist.com/article/mg25634132-300-why-emotions-can-feel-so-painful-and-what-it-means-for-painkillers/ accessed 4 January 2023

Chapter Seven

James Clear, *Atomic Habits. Tiny Changes, Remarkable Results.*
(Penguin 2018)

Chapter Eight

Connor Wood, 'Why Imitation Is at the Heart of Being
Human' 23 January 2020, *Berkeley University*, https://
greatergood.berkeley.edu/article/item/why_imitation_
is_at_the_heart_of_being_human, accessed 22
September 2023

Dr Alokananda Rudra 'Why many women with autism
and ADHD aren't diagnosed until adulthood – and
what to do if you think you're one of them', Durham
University Blog 22 April 2022 https://www.durham.
ac.uk/research/current/thought-leadership/women-
with-autism-adhd-arent-diagnosed-until-adulthood/,
accessed 22 October 2023

Anna Quintal, 'Why neurodivergent women are diagnosed
with ADHD and autism later in life, and what this
means for their careers' 18 August 2022, The Brain
Charity Blog, https://www.thebraincharity.org.uk/
neurodivergent-women-adhd-autism-adults/, accessed
21 August 2023

Author unknown, 'Women In Autism' 2023, Autism.org
blog https://autism.org/women-in-autism/, accessed 29
October 2023

Dr Jim, 'Understanding the Strong Connection Between Entrepreneurs and ADHD' Fast Braiin Blog, undated, Understanding the Strong Connection Between Entrepreneurs and ADHD – FastBraiin, accessed 12 August 2023

Robert D. Austin and Gary P. Pisano 'Neurodiversity as a Competitive Advantage – Why you should embrace it in your workforce'. *Harvard Business Review magazine* May-June 2017, accessed 14 August 2023. https://hbr.org/2017/05/neurodiversity-as-a-competitive-advantage

Thriiver, 'Spotlight on Neurodiverse Teams' Make A Difference Media Blog, 20 September 2023 https://makeadifference.media/culture/spotlight-on-the-benefits-of-neurodiverse-teams/ accessed 29 November 2023

Chris Packham, *'Inside Our Autistic Minds'*, episode one, BBC 2 Television 14 February 2023 https://www.bbc.co.uk/iplayer/episode/p0bbnjvx/inside-our-autistic-minds-series-1-episode-1, accessed 16 February 2023

FURTHER INFORMATION/RESOURCES

Future Life Meditation

Jason Stephenson *'Spoken Meditation: Your Ideal Life, The Law Of Attraction: Goal Setting Visualization'* 2014 https://youtu.be/J11_JxqSJlE?si=h1t7oqJueURorkYl accessed April 2020

EXAMPLES OF CORE VALUES

Authenticity	Faith	Optimism
Achievement	Freedom	Pride
Adventure	Friendships	Positivity
Authority	Fun	Popularity
Autonomy	Growth	Recognition
Balance	Happiness	Religion
Beauty	Honesty	Reputation
Boldness	Humour	Respect
Compassion	Influence	Responsibility
Challenge	Integrity	Security
Connection	Inclusivity	Self-Respect
Community	Justice	Service
Competency	Kindness	Spirituality
Contribution	Knowledge	Stability
Courage	Leadership	Success
Creativity	Learning	Status
Curiosity	Love	Trustworthiness
Determination	Loyalty	Wealth
Fairness	Meaningful Work	Wisdom
	Openness	

ACKNOWLEDGEMENTS

I started writing a book almost two decades ago, although it was a very different kind of book. I never got past the first few pages before I lost interest. I returned to it numerous times, only to get distracted and lose interest again....

This has been an altogether different experience. My first draft poured out of me in less than three months. I knew this was the book I was supposed to write and I couldn't get it out of my head quickly enough. Notice I said 'the first draft' came quickly. The editing process has not been quite so easy breezy for my AuDHD brain, but thanks to my epic publishing team, we got there!

I'd first like to thank my parents for their support since my late diagnosis and for believing in me as I launched The Autistic Joyologist and wrote this book.

To my mum, you've been with me every step of the way. I know it hasn't been easy learning about the struggles and challenges I kept hidden for so long. The grace with which you have committed to getting to know me as my true neuro-divergent self has been incredible and I am truly grateful for your support and understanding.

I want to express my heartfelt thanks to Mark Leruste. Your inspiration was the spark that ignited my journey as The Autistic Joyologist. Without that, the pages of this book would remain blank and I would still be in the shadows. Working with you, reading *Glow in The Dark*, and joining your *Own Your Story* program enabled me to find the courage and fire to follow my heart and share my story with the world.

Thank you to the neurodivergent women I've connected with along the way. Your openness and honesty have taught me so much and pushed me to continue to learn, grow and develop to provide strategies and support that benefit our community.

To all the women who have reached out and shared that my story helped you discover your neurodivergence and how you felt seen for the first time, thank you. You continue to remind me to keep sharing stories to spark new conversations and a more profound sense of connection.

Thank you to the team at Authors & Co. for believing in me and offering the support and flexibility I needed to make this dream a reality. Writing a book as an autistic ADHD'er hasn't been easy, but you've made the whole experience fun and accessible, for which I am truly grateful.

Finally, to my little cat, Maverick! You'll never understand the support you provided through your encouraging head bumps, soothing purrs, and much-needed cuddles when fatigue and frustration hit. I promise to forever show my appreciation with Dreamies and tummy rubs!

THE AUTHOR

Nikki Butler – Founder

Nikki Butler is an award-winning entrepreneur and founder of The Autistic Joyologist.

Dedicated to supporting neurodivergent and neuro-curious women in creating lives that resonate with their unique identities, Nikki believes that finding balance, personal fulfilment and success without sacrificing who we are is the key to long-term happiness and success.

Diagnosed as autistic and ADHD in her mid-forties, Nikki transformed her personal challenges into a mission to eradicate outdated stereotypes and stigmas about being neurodivergent.

She is a celebrated voice in neurodivergent entrepreneurship. With guest spots on platforms like BBC Radio and articles in StartUp Magazine and The Industry Leaders, she draws on over twenty years of leadership, entrepreneurship and a lifetime of personal experience. Her work challenges the norms and offers a fresh blueprint for living a life where being different is your greatest asset.

Nikki firmly believes that neurodiversity is vital to what makes humanity rich and varied, however, society has long clung to a narrow definition of 'normal,' building systems favouring this norm and excluding those who don't fit.

She argues that it's time to challenge these outdated stereotypes and stigmas. Neurodivergence isn't a deviation to be corrected but a spectrum to be understood and embraced. She advocates for a shift towards a society that supports every individual, recognising that thriving is not about conforming but embracing and supporting all forms of human diversity.

Before starting The Autistic Joyologist, Nikki founded a specialist skin and scar practice and worked in private practice solicitors and corporate legal management for over ten years before becoming an entrepreneur. She brings a wealth of experience from her professional pursuits alongside her lived experiences, enabling her to connect deeply with others.

Her approach is refreshing and unique, combining her sharp business acumen with her ability to spark deeply personal insights and learnings. She enables others to resonate and connect with her in a profound and life-changing way.

Through The Autistic Joyologist, Nikki helps women stop living in constant overwhelm, people-pleasing and burnout and start living aligned, balanced and fulfilling lives that bring them joy and happiness on their terms.

As a business strategy consultant, she guides entrepreneurs and business owners towards success by helping them create bespoke strategies that complement their unique skills and brains. Her approach fosters a business culture that champions accessibility and provides empowering support for all team members.

Away from work, Nikki enjoys silversmithing, strength training and being outside in the fresh air. Ever curious, you'll always find her studying for something!

Nikki is available for speaking engagements, interviews, podcasts, guest writing/blogging and expert training/workshops. Nikki also offers business strategy consulting services for entrepreneurs, business owners and organisations to help them develop/grow their businesses and create an inclusive diversity-focused culture.

YOU CAN REACH NIKKI AT:

Email: hello@autisticjoyologist.co.uk

Facebook/ Instagram: @autisticjoyologist

LinkedIn: @nikkibutlerautisticjoyologist

Website: www.autisticjoyologist.co.uk

www.ingramcontent.com/pod-product-compliance
Lightning Source LLC
Chambersburg PA
CBHW020719080726
47818CB00024B/320/J